Discovering Architecture

HOW THE WORLD'S GREAT BUILDINGS
WERE DESIGNED AND BUILT

PHILIP JODIDIO

UNIVERSE

Discovering Architecture

How the World's Great Buildings Were Designed and Built

(PAGES 1, 3 AND 5)
Guggenheim Bilbao
Bilbao, Spain, 1997

Published by Universe Publishing
A Division of Rizzoli International Publications, Inc.
300 Park Avenue South
New York, NY 10010
www.rizzoliusa.com

© 2013 Universe Publishing

Book Designer: Kevin Osborn, Research & Design, Ltd., Arlington, Virginia
Project Director: James O. Muschett
Caption Text: Elizabeth M. Dowling, PhD., and Robin H. Prater

Photography Credits

Album / Art Resource, NY: pp. 9, 158, 161
Alinari / Art Resource, NY: pp. 114
Art Resource, NY: pp. 198–199
© Iwan Baan: pp. 256, 259
© Bauhaus Dessau Foundation: pp. 186
bpk, Berlin (Photo: Jürgen Hohmuth) / Art Resource, NY: pp. 152, 155, 156–157
© Brent C. Brolin / Art Resource, NY: pp. 180, 183
Steven Brooke Studios: back cover, pp. 19, 148
Stéphane Compoint: pp. 8, 250, 253, 254–255
Leonardo Finotti: pp. 22, 208, 211, 212–213
Fondation Le Corbusier: pp. 200
Werner Forman / Art Resource, NY: pp. 96, 99
Dennis Gilbert and Gianni Berengo Gardin: pp. 242, 245
HIP / Art Resource, NY: pp. 13, 116, 119
Andrea Jemolo / Scala / Art Resource, NY: pp. 20, 21, 190, 193, 204, 207
Jeff Laitila: pp. 16, 95
Erich Lessing / Art Resource, NY: pp. 10, 14, 20, 22, 29, 32, 35, 40, 43, 44–45, 67, 77,
     86–87, 102, 105, 113, 156, 166, 169, 170–171, 176, 179, 203, 228, 229
Christopher Little: pp. 21, 194, 197
Mitsuo Matsuoka: pp. 232, 235
Nimatallah / Art Resource, NY: pp. 114–115
Gianni Dagli Orti / The Art Archive at Art Resource, NY: pp. 82, 85
© Musée de l'Armée/Dist. RMN-Grand Palais / Art Resource, NY: pp. 18, 141, 142–143
Ralph Richter/Esto/arkitekturphoto: front cover, pp. 1, 3, 5, 24, 246, 249
© RMN-Grand Palais / Art Resource, NY: pp. 16, 23, 120, 123, 236, 239, 240–241
Scala / Art Resource, NY: pp. 12, 13, 54, 57, 58–59, 60, 63, 68, 71, 72–73, 86, 106, 109
Scala / White Images / Art Resource, NY: pp. 11, 49
SEF / Art Resource, NY: pp. 11, 50, 53, 100–101, 151, 162, 165
Ezra Stoller © Esto: pp. 214, 217, 221
Tim Street-Porter: pp. 218
Courtesy Sydney Opera House: pp. 222, 225, 226–227
Universal Images Group / Art Resource, NY: pp. 172, 175
Vanni / Art Resource, NY: pp. 10, 15, 17, 30–31, 26, 39, 81, 91, 92, 100, 124, 127,
     128–129, 130, 133, 134, 137, 144, 147, 170, 184–185, 189

2012 2013 2014 2015 / 10 9 8 7 6 5 4 3 2 1

Printed in China

ISBN-13: 978-0-7893-2707-9

Library of Congress Catalog Control Number: 2013934875

Contents

Discovering Architecture

Millau Viaduct, Millau,
France, 2004

FOR VARIOUS REASONS, architecture has often been considered an art, and as such, it is sometimes seen as a preserve of the elite. Books or magazines about architecture tend to address themselves to those who already know, the cognoscenti of the built form. And yet great works of architecture, those that last sometimes for centuries, are buildings or structures that serve again and again. True, great buildings may be reserved for the use of a certain elite, but more often than not, they are places where power or the world of the spirit is expressed. The architecture that remains and is preserved usually has an impact on a great number of people, whence the basic fallacy of architectural elitism. Thousands upon thousands and sometimes millions of people have used the buildings that are published in this book. Only a few are residences, and even those are sometimes symbolically significant because they have housed rulers. Churches and mosques, temples and towers are buildings that stand out and symbolize faith or power, be it temporal or ecclesiastical.

Architecture, as it is defined for the purposes of this book, goes beyond buildings to include great public spaces like Red Square in Moscow. It includes works that might best be qualified as triumphs of engineering, from the Great Wall of China to the Millau Bridge in France. It is only progressively, beginning with the Italian Renaissance, or some Gothic works, that the name of the designer of a structure has come to be retained and remembered. Early buildings, surely, had a concept that one or more people imagined, but when a Gothic cathedral is built over centuries, individual identity is subsumed in a collective work of faith. The architect as "genius" emerges with figures such as Alberti, Brunelleschi, and Michelangelo. Even great churches like the Sagrada Familia in Barcelona are now identified with their creator, even if the completion of this nineteenth-century edifice is not yet clearly programmed. The visitor to the Forbidden City in Beijing does not naturally ask for the name of the architect. Rather, it is clear that this great palace is the willful creation of generations of rulers who have added or subtracted elements according to their needs and desires. The same is of course true of Versailles.

So, too, the notion of the preservation and restoration of architecture is a relatively recent one. Keeping vestiges of the past was often the very opposite of what those in power wanted. And so Catholic churches were usually built on the site of Roman temples, as if to show that the past was no longer of interest. Great buildings serve a purpose and evolve over time, even at the expense of erasing the achievements of an earlier era. Kings and democratically elected rulers of France have modified the Louvre over the centuries, and it is this remarkable layering of history that identifies one place as the heart of a nation.

The Convention Concerning the Protection of the World Cultural and Natural Heritage was adopted by the General Conference of UNESCO on November 16, 1972. As of 2012, 745 cultural sites around the world have been listed by the agency as worthy of preservation. Many of the buildings in this book are on the UNESCO World Heritage List, which certainly is a precious source of information and does serve to protect monuments that might otherwise be swept aside by urban development. But the UNESCO World Heritage List is an indication of a fundamental change in how old buildings are viewed. Whereas in the past, a structure would stand or be modified only on the basis of how useful it was, now architecture can be preserved in whatever state it has reached modern times, most likely never again to be rebuilt, modified, or modernized. In this sense, the great architecture of the past has entered its museum phase, when tourists file by to imagine the glory that was Rome or Beijing in another time. This transition to a museum phase is a broadly based sociological phenomenon linked to the ease of travel in today's world. It is also the result of fundamental changes in the way things are designed and built. Workers can no longer individually carve stones to make a flying buttress, and only the church can still imagine a building that takes a century or more to complete. Times have changed, and thus the very way we look at the architecture of the past has evolved.

Sagrada Familia Basilica,
Barcelona, Spain, 1883

Finally, whereas in the past, powerful rulers or heads of churches could almost singlehandedly decide to build or to raze a great building, today democratization, capitalist impulses, and international organizations like UNESCO all have their word to say. Reducing cost has become a leitmotif of architecture, surely not the best way to build a masterpiece. The architecture of centuries past, sometimes seen as proof of the historic continuity of the greatness of a nation, is placed in a state of suspended animation, a kind of cryogenic postcard existence that means that some significant buildings will never be truly alive again.

Hagia Sofia,
Istanbul, Turkey, 537

Todaiji Temple,
Nara, Japan, 8th century

Perhaps the most important observation that can be gleaned from the fifty examples selected for this book—all dating from the Christian era to the present—is that each and every one of them is invested with life. Far from being curious unapproachable works of art, these examples of architecture are the very places in which our civilizations are founded; they are the crucible not only of esthetics and culture but also of politics, religion, and history. As such, great architecture is by no means the preserve of an elite; it is the tangible proof of where we come from and who we are.

The buildings in this book are organized, to the greatest extent possible, by their date of completion. Of course, many buildings, especially the older ones, have had various functions and forms and cannot be dated with such precision. This is in fact the great conundrum of architectural restoration of ancient buildings. Which Versailles does one restore—that of Louis XIV (1638–1715) or that, a world apart, of Louis-Philippe (1773–1850)?

Cathedral, Mosque, Museum, Temple

A first concrete example of the different avatars of a single building is Hagia Sophia (Istanbul, Turkey; 537). It served as an Eastern Orthodox cathedral, a Catholic cathedral, an imperial mosque, and finally, since 1935, as a museum. Located on the site of two earlier churches, the basilica was built on the order of Justinian I, the Byzantine emperor from 527 to 565. It was inaugurated by the emperor and Eutychius, ecumenical patriarch of Constantinople, on December 27, 537. Ancient by the standards of any existing building, Hagia Sophia contains even older architectural elements, such as eight Corinthian columns brought from Baalbek on the order of the emperor and used in construction. Hovering above Hagia Sophia, its dome, with an interior height of 182.4 feet (55.6 meters), is a symbol retained for many churches, mosques, and government buildings over time. The dome can be seen as a symbol of the heavens, or even of the human skull, that which renders life possible.

The dome of the heavens does not seem to have been as much of a preoccupation in the Far East. Todaiji Temple (Nara, Japan; 752) is one of the great monuments of Buddhism. Here, the extent of faith and the importance of Nara as the brief capital of Japan were expressed in the construction of temples and, in the case of Todaiji, of a likeness of Buddha, housed in the largest wooden building in the world. Forty-nine feet (15 meters) high, the Great Buddha was inaugurated in 752. Fires and earthquakes got the better of parts of the temple complex, but most of them were rebuilt, again and again, as required. Aside from the main building that houses the sculpture, Todaiji Temple today includes seven other structures that are classified in Japan as national treasures. This architecture and the very mood of Nara are still remarkable symbols of a faith that bound a country together. Todajiji was responsible for all the other Buddhist temples of Japan, a measure of its significance that can still be felt today.

The construction of Chartres Cathedral started in 1145, but it was rebuilt after a fire in 1194. The cathedral was consecrated in 1260 in the presence of King Louis IX of France. Described by UNESCO as a "high point of French Gothic art," Chartres might be considered the Christian equivalent of a temple like Todaiji, a center of culture and, indeed, of civilization. Chartres is about 50 miles (80 kilometers) from Paris and was a Roman Catholic diocese as early as the third century, with at least four churches having been built on the same site as the present cathedral before the twelfth century. This type of successive rebuilding, for reasons of fire or simply to create a greater and better church, is also typical of many important Christian monuments. A given site is considered for centuries to be a propitious one for a building that is an expression of faith. With its flying buttresses and structural design, Chartres allowed for exceptionally large stained-glass windows, including three large, round "rose" windows depicting the Last Judgment (west), the Virgin (north), and Christ (south). The great nave surely is a reminiscence of the forests of an era before history, an architectural recreation of a space more ancient than recorded time. Reaching back before history and forward to the present, a monument like Chartres connects people and their cultures through time; it is a real, still-living link to the beliefs that founded Europe and much of the Western world.

Chartres Cathedral,
Chartres, France, 1193–1250

Cambodia is one of only two countries in the world (with Afghanistan) to have a building on its national flag. In the case of Afghanistan, a generic mosque, in fact a representation of faith, holds the center of the flag. For Cambodia, the monument represented is the temple of Angkor Wat (Siem Reap, Cambodia; 1150). One of roughly a thousand temples in the region of Angkor, Angkor Wat, dedicated to Vishnu, was the largest Hindu temple in the world, and its form is felt to be a symbolic representation of Hindu cosmology. Long abandoned, the complex of Angkor was brought to world attention by the French explorer Henri Mouhot (1826–1861), who wrote, "One of these temples—a rival to that of Solomon, and erected by some ancient Michelangelo—might take an honorable place beside our most beautiful buildings. It is grander than anything left to us by Greece or Rome." The name of the Khmer

Angkor Wat,
Siem Reap, Cambodia, 12th century

"Michelangelo" is not known, nor might it be likely that Angkor Wat was built to the designs of a single person. Rather, it stands not only as a symbol of earthly power but as a representation of the universe as it was understood by its builders. Many learned studies have been published about the forms and sculptures of Angkor Wat, but its physical grandeur can be felt by all who enter its outer walls. This place was made holy by those who believe. The "architects" of Angkor Wat and all the faithful who have come to pray have invested it with an authenticity and a reality that cannot be denied. The spirit of country, its history and pride, is visible on its flag, the outline of Angkor Wat's towering forms.

The Importance of Public Space

City squares may not generally be considered works of architecture in and of themselves, and yet, when they are successful, these public spaces give importance to the architecture that surrounds them and also constitute the very substance of the life of a city. There are of course examples of squares that have been willfully designed by a single architect or planner—the Plano Piloto for Brasília created by Lúcio Costa in 1957 comes to mind. The Eixo Monumental (Monumental Axis) of the city is the green spine that runs between the government buildings, both a great public space and an essential element of urban design. Pierre Charles L'Enfant's 1791 master plan for Washington, D.C., is of course a precursor of Costa's green spine.

Piazza del Campo,
Siena, Italy, 14th century

The Piazza del Campo (Siena, Italy; 1280–1350) is the main public space of the historic center of Siena in Tuscany. The unusual semicircular shell shape of the square is formed by the Palazzo Pubblico, built between 1297 and 1308 on the lower side, and a series of private palaces of the same height along the upper edge (*palazzi signorili*). Prior to the thirteenth century the area of the piazza was the marketplace for a group of closely grouped towns. The square was paved between 1327 and 1349 under the auspices of the Council of Nine (Governo dei Nove), who ruled Siena from 1287 to 1355. More than the intervention of any single architect, the unity and beauty of the Piazza del Campo is undoubtedly due to town regulations that imposed restrictions of height and style on any building near the square.

Moscow's Red Square, which lies in front of the Kremlin, was created on the orders of Ivan the Great (1440–1505). An area 768 feet (234 meters) wide was cleared of all construction near the new walls of the Kremlin. St. Basil's Cathedral (1554–60), built on orders of Ivan the Terrible (1530–1584), is at its head. The major streets of Russia's capital find their point of origin in the square, highlighting its symbolic significance, which was confirmed in modern times by the many official ceremonies held there, including during the Soviet years. One of the world's great public spaces, Red Square is an incarnation of Russia itself; its history, both ancient and recent, is summed up in its buildings, which have evolved over time, including the modern reconstruction of a church that had been demolished. Protected by Russia, but also by UNESCO and its very weight in history, Red Square was thus the creation of the tsars, a grand square where more or less despotic rulers have made themselves visible from year to year. Individual architects have contributed to its components, but the square itself surpasses the inventiveness of individuals to become the symbolic heart of a country. This might be called a collective act of architectural design, spanning centuries, or it might be seen for what it is, the expression of a nation and its history. Great architecture goes beyond stones and decoration, creating a place where great events are played out and where thought is formed.

Red Square,
Moscow, Russia, 17th century

Rome's Piazza del Campidoglio (1546), located on the Capitoline Hill, was inhabited and built on from the earliest times of Rome, the location of a number of temples, one of which was dedicated to Jupiter. The seat of city government in the Middle Ages, the square lost its grandeur over time but had an alignment facing the Roman Forum. With its palaces in poor condition, Pope Paul III (1468–1549) gave orders to rebuild the square on the occasion of a planned visit of the Holy Roman Emperor Charles V. Redesigning the square so that it would face St. Peter's Basilica, Michelangelo Buonarroti gave the sloping, trapezoidal space an undeniable grandeur. He also designed or redesigned the major buildings, including the Palazzo Nuovo, whose construction was completed after his death in 1564. Because it was the site of the Temple of Jupiter at a time when Rome really was the "center of the world," reference has been made to the Campidoglio as being the *caput mundi*, or "head of the world." The oval or, more precisely, egglike form of Michelangelo's design for the paving of the square, placing an equestrian statue of Marcus Aurelius (then thought to represent Constantine, the first Christian leader of Rome) facing St. Peter's, is redolent with symbolism. Axial symmetry is sought, and it is clearly suggested that the new world, that of Christendom, in a sense starts here.

Piazza del Campidoglio,
Rome, Italy, 16th century

Centers of Power, Symbols of Triumph

It would seem that the world has many centers because, far to the east, the Forbidden City of Beijing was built in the fifteenth century (1407–20) as the seat of power of the emperors of China who ruled "All under heaven."

Forbidden City,
Beijing, China, 1420

Great Wall of China,
3rd century B.C. to 17th century

This axial and symmetrical complex covers more than 178 acres (72 hectares). It faces Tiananmen Square, the third largest city square in the world, and the location of the mausoleum of Mao Tse-tung. Twenty-four emperors sat in majesty in a complex that includes no fewer than 980 buildings and nearly 10,000 rooms. Converted into the Palace Museum in 1925, the complex is considered to be one of the largest and best-preserved examples of wooden palace architecture in the world. Whether it be within its walls symbolic of the exalted power of the emperors, or on Tiananmen Square, the site of parades and at least one noted revolt, the place of burial, too, of China's first Communist "emperor," the Forbidden City is another example of collective architecture born of the ruler's orders. Because so many workers had to be mobilized in a relatively short period, only absolute power, with all the abuses that it implies, could give rise to such a monument of architecture.

China's Great Wall (220 B.C.–A.D. 1644) is an example of military or defensive architecture whose construction spanned more than eighteen hundred years. With its total length of 12,427 miles (20,000 kilometers), it is by far the longest man-made structure. Its style and materials of course varied over time, but it is the continuity of purpose and basic form that makes the Great Wall a work of architecture like no other. It is an expression of history, a barrier against not only invading Barbarians but also threats to the culture of China. It might be noted that by the time the first Western accounts of the Great Wall emerged, as late as 1605, European countries had long thought themselves to be the greatest powers and sources of civilization on the planet. By the time of the reign of the Emperor Wudi (140–87 B.C.), the Great Wall already stretched for a length of about 3,728 miles (6,000 kilometers), from the Bohai Sea to Dunhuang. The Middle Kingdom was capable of realizations that even imperial Rome could not surpass. Aside from anecdotal evidence such as the voyages of Marco Polo (1254–1324), who makes no reference to the Great Wall, Europe was in large part blissfully ignorant of the achievements of the civilizations of the East until much more recent times.

The Italian Renaissance surely does mark a transition in architecture because of the emergence of individual artists and creators of genius, who left their names to posterity. In 1502, the architect Donato Bramante (1444–1514) was commissioned by Ferdinand of Aragon and Isabella of Castile to build a small structure called the Tempietto in the cloister of the Church of San Pietro in Montorio (Rome, Italy; 1502–10). Thought to be the very site of the crucifixion of St. Peter, the centrally planned, circular Tempietto is related in its conception to Roman and early Christian *martyria*, monuments erected as memorials or to commemorate events of particular significance. The Tempietto is surely related in its geometric proportions to the thinking of the time, which delved into the art and architecture of the ancient world. It was in approximately 1490 that Leonardo da Vinci made his celebrated drawing of a figure inscribed in a circle, together with an Italian translation of the relevant text by Vitruvius (80–15 B.C.), which posits that a well-proportioned man fits, with arms and legs extended, into perfect geometric forms—the circle and square. More precisely, Vitruvius wrote, "without symmetry and proportion no temple can have a regular plan; that is, it must have an exact proportion worked out after the fashion of the limbs of the finely shaped human body." It may be that Bramante met Leonardo in 1504 in Rome and that the small Tempietto is the expression of thoughts that go back to Roman times and forward to the present. Geometric simplicity, albeit of a less philosophical origin, is a hallmark of most modern architecture.

Tempietto, San Pietro in Montorio, Rome, Italy, 1510

Lines of influence can be drawn from Bramante to Andrea Palladio (1508–1580), one of the most influential architects in history. In his *Four Books of Architecture* (1570), Palladio wrote: "Since Bramante was the first to make known that good and beautiful architecture which had been hidden from the times of the ancients until now, I thought it reasonable that his work should be placed amongst those of the ancients." His own Villa Almerico Capra, also called La Rotonda (Vicenza, Italy; 1571), has a symmetrical plan with a central round hall and a dome, inscribed in the square form of the house itself, with four porticos with Ionic-style columns. Clearly the inspiration of the temple, be it ancient or Christian like the Tempietto, is not far removed from this work of domestic architecture. This is significant in that it represents the translation of the conception of more symbolic and "public" monuments to the private sphere. Just as the architect was becoming an individual whose name would be remembered, so, too, the private client was beginning to aspire to the sort of "immortality" previously reserved essentially to rulers and popes. In fact, the central dome of the villa was completed only in 1606 with designs by Vincenzo Scamozzi, and was modeled on the dome of the Pantheon in Rome. Thus, even a work by the great Palladio presents features that were designed by others, as is most often the case of great buildings. More than one hand created this masterpiece.

Villa Almerico Capra, La Rotonda, Vicenza, Italy, 1571

Endless Perspectives

Experts in architecture might be hesitant to include a garden in a book that should be about buildings. And yet, one of the real measures of the greatness of architecture is the way in which it makes use of space, or rather perhaps how it creates a place, which is used and preserved over the centuries. The garden at Ryoan-ji temple (Kyoto, Japan; ca. 1500) is a *karesansui,* or Japanese dry landscape garden (also called "withered landscapes"). This is to say that unlike most gardens it is made up only of mineral elements. The garden consists of raked gravel and fifteen moss-covered stones, placed so that from any angle only fourteen can be seen at once. It is said that only when one attains enlightenment in the spiritual sense does it become possible to see the fifteenth stone. This is a concept related to Zen Buddhism, but it is also an expression of what makes a place remarkable. The garden at Ryoan-ji exists only to be observed; it is not possible to walk through it, only to sit on the long, smoothly worn wooden planks of the temple and to contemplate its forms. The garden can also be seen as a metaphor for existence, or perhaps for the universe, with the permanent, ineffable ambiguity of life expressed through the careful placement of stones. What would architecture look like if it, too, attained a state of enlightenment? Surely something like this garden.

The Palace of Versailles (Versailles, France; ca. 1670) might seem to be at the diametrical opposite of Ryoan-ji. It is nothing if not extravagant, the very expression of the self-perceived glory of France. The palace was a showplace for the authority and culture of the French monarchy, and of the "Sun King" (Louis XIV) in particular, but it also served a political purpose, obliging the sometimes-rebellious nobles to be grouped around the king, rather than plotting against him elsewhere. The Château de Versailles as it exists today has a floor area of 721,180 square feet (67,000 square meters) and no fewer than 2,300 rooms. The most talented architects, artists, furniture designers, and landscape designers of the period collaborated to make Versailles an expression not only of individual power, but of a time. The landscape architect André Le Nôtre (1613–1700), for example, created the great perspectives that are the most visible element of the gardens of Versailles. Curiously, where interiors are covered with gold, the gardens might be seen as an expression of minimalism, a kind of "land art" well before its time. The real art of Le Nôtre was his capacity to use earth, water, and sky to create an image of power that extends beyond the horizon, as though real power might consist more in the absolute mastery of space rather than in political and military might. What is obvious is that elements of Le Nôtre's design still exist, long after the kings of France went the way of collapse and ruin.

Ryoan-ji Temple,
Kyoto, Japan, 16th century

Hall of Mirrors, Chateau de Versailles,
Versailles, France, 17th century

The Judgment of Time

Sometimes the significance of a work of architecture is revealed only over time, and with the benefit of hindsight. Such might be the case of the Katsura Imperial Villa (Kyoto, Japan; 1620–63). Katsura was all but abandoned by the time the German architect Bruno Taut (1880–1938) arrived in Japan in 1933 at the invitation of the Japanese Association for International Architecture. Such was its state of neglect that on November 4, 1935, Taut wrote, "I can claim to be the 'discoverer' of Katsura." Taut and then Le Corbusier and Gropius were fascinated by Katsura's "modernity." They saw its undecorated orthogonal and modular spaces as parallels to contemporary modernism, going so far as to identify Katsura as a "historical" example of modernity. The modernists saw what they wanted to see in Katsura—the Mondrian-like simplicity of certain designs—while looking less at its rustic side, or at the "complexity and contradiction" that lie in almost every aspect of the buildings and gardens. More recently, Japanese critics and architects, at first strongly influenced by Taut, took up their own analysis of Katsura. Arata Isozaki wrote about the fundamental ambiguity of the palace. As he says, "I have not been able to see the Katsura in the same light as the modernists once did. They selected what they wanted from the Katsura, its transparence, its functionally designed space. I have viewed it rather as a great mixture, as deeply ambiguous. I have taken its evolution as resulting from accidents and a certain opacity of design." Clearly, Katsura is a secular masterpiece, an alliance of architecture and the arts of the garden or of decor. Like most great works, it can be read or understood by different visitors in different ways, and it remains a fundamental expression of Japan, or rather of universal culture. Long reserved for the use of Japanese nobility, Katsura does not participate in the same kind of extensive use over time that has confirmed the status of other works of great architecture. This is an essentially private building and garden that reached a level of perfection and beauty that can readily be understood almost four centuries later.

Many great works can be seen as representations of faith and more—models in a sense of the universe itself. In this, works of architecture share, at their highest level, a fundamental similarity with other forms of art. The greatest works are very often ambiguous but do suggest the existence of a higher order, or perhaps a deep connection to the realities of this world. The Taj Mahal (Agra, Uttar Pradesh, India; 1648) is one of these places. Its gardens clearly represent the four rivers of paradise. The Taj Mahal itself is elevated on a 313.3 foot (95.5 meter) square plinth at the dis-

Katsura Imperial Villa,
Kyoto, Japan, 17th century

Taj Mahal,
Agra, India, 1648

tant end of the garden. The great dome that dominates the structure is placed in the center of this square and forms a perfect circle. It has frequently been written that in the symbolism of Islam, a square represents man, and a circle the divine. Leonardo's Vitruvian Man is of course inscribed in a circle and a square, giving a humanist interpretation to shapes used by the Mughals to other ends. And yet years and continents apart, art and architecture fuse around the same essential forms. Pure geometric forms, in particular the circle, are said to be "perfect" and therefore surely related to the divine as much or more than any more complex human construct. Religiously oriented architecture, from the Tempietto to the Taj Mahal and beyond, calls on these forms in their relation to human affairs and events, as though to conjure up the protective divinity, to assimilate a building and therefore its builder with eternity.

Les Invalides,
Paris, France, 1674

History combines itself with significant monuments in many ways. Churches often built on the site of other churches or earlier temples are one example of this kind of layering of events that occurs on a single site. Another is the ways in which important buildings are used and what their architectural sources of inspiration may be. The Hôtel national des Invalides (Paris, France; 1674) is located on the axis of the Alexander III Bridge on the Left Bank of the Seine in Paris. It is one of the most recognizable buildings in the city because of its 351 foot (107 meter) high dome, which was modeled to a large extent on that of St. Peter's in Rome. Whatever its source, Les Invalides has also influenced the form of major buildings that came after it, such as the dome of the United States Capitol in Washington, D.C. (Thomas Walter; 1866); the U.S. Naval Academy Chapel (Annapolis, Maryland; 1908); and San Francisco City Hall (1915). Founded as a veteran's hospital with a cathedral within its walls, Les Invalides may be better known as the resting place of Napoleon I. Louis Visconti (1791–1853), who would later work on the Louvre, designed the tomb in which the emperor's remains were placed in 1861. The openly visible red quartzite tomb is lifted up on a green granite base, located directly under the great dome designed by Jules Hardouin-Mansart. Thus a church was made into a mausoleum and became irrevocably associated with a part of French history that had nothing to do with its creation.

Past Glories, Modern Needs

America enters the lists of great buildings only in the eighteenth century, and quite obviously European influences played a significant role in early structures of note such as Monticello (near Charlottesville, Virginia; 1784). Monticello is of course associated with its designer and owner, the third president of the United States, Thomas Jefferson. The hilltop location and natural setting of Monticello, as well as its architecture, is said to be influenced by Palladio's Villa Rotonda (Villa Almerico Capra, Vicenza, Italy; 1571), and its basically cruciform plan is similar to that of Chiswick House (London, England; 1729). Monticello, with its domed form and sense of geometry, does lie clearly in the continuity of Palladio and, before him, the Renaissance figures such as Bramante who referred back to Vitruvius. Proportions and a nobility of spirit are thus firmly associated with an exceptional private residence, a kind of temple for modern times. In the case of Jefferson, author of the Declaration of Independence, the nobility of spirit is one that he clearly translated into the institutions of the new country. Democracy and eventually equality (though Jefferson was an owner of slaves) are the clear messages that this architecture can convey. Though other locations might well vie for that title, Monticello could be seen as a monument to a man and to a country he helped create. It is finally imbued with a spirit that flowed from Vitruvius to Palladio, by way of England and France, a clear new architecture of carefully calculated dimensions, made to elevate and glorify the spirit.

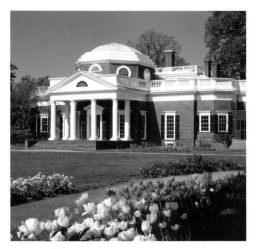

Monticello,
Charlottesville, Virginia, USA, 1782

Jefferson was at least indirectly a promoter of the Greek revival style of architecture, even before many significant neoclassical buildings were erected in Europe. One significant example of this trend is the Altes Museum (Berlin, Germany; 1830), designed by Karl Friedrich Schinkel (1781–1841). Its long facade with eighteen Ionic columns and its interior dome inspired by the Pantheon are an expression of the nobility of art and education as it was put forward in Germany by Wilhelm von Humboldt (1767–1835), a philosopher and founder of the University of Berlin. Art, education, and consequently architecture were no longer to be reserved for an elite, but for a broadening class of newly empowered middle- to upper-class citizens.

The Industrial Paradigm

The design of buildings has always been related to the science of engineering. Once an empirical form of knowledge, engineering became progressively more precise. The Eiffel Tower (Paris, France; 1889) remained the tallest building in the world from 1889 to 1930, when it was surpassed by New York's Chrysler Building. Built as the entrance arch to the 1889 Universal Exhibition, it is named after the French engineer Gustave Eiffel, whose own Compagnie des Éstablissments Eiffel built it. Though it may well be that Eiffel and his colleagues still used relatively empirical methods for the design, its rapid construction using industrial

Eiffel Tower,
Paris, France, 1889

methods and, indeed, its symbolic import make it a first real symbol of the industrial age. More than two million persons visited it in the course of the exhibition. The Eiffel Tower remains the most-visited paying monument in the world, although it fulfills little function except offering a spectacular view of the French capital. Unlike other monuments or squares that have witnessed the very real passage of historic events, the Eiffel Tower is like a great sculpture that announces the modern era, and in this, as well as its unexpected longevity, it deserves to enter even the briefest of lists of great architectural achievements.

It has been seen that shifts in the history of architecture and, indeed, in the sociological changes in the Western world first admitted that a private residence could take on the trappings formerly reserved for church and state. By the time the Eiffel Tower was built, and in the years following, it was industry itself that brazenly assumed that it, too, could have its temples, its places of worship. The AEG Turbine Factory (Berlin, Germany; 1910) was designed by Peter Behrens and the engineer Karl Bernhard for an electrical company that acquired the right to make use of the patents of Thomas Edison. Behrens created an unembarrassed ode to the industry, calling on Greek and Egyptian temple design in order to glorify the emerging power of electricity. In philosophical terms, Behrens believed in the power of art to transform and dignify everyday life. Rather than glorifying the machine, as some later modern architects did with force, Behrens sought to impose the victory of art over banality. Even a factory could be a place of dignity, where architecture at its most evolved level could play a role.

During the same period, railway stations, which were the embodiment of the emerging era of public transport, took on the air of vast temples. Grand Central Terminal (New York, New York, United States; 1913) was hailed by the *New York Times* as "not only the greatest station in the United States, but the greatest station, of any type, in the world." With its vast main concourse decorated by noted French artists of the time, the station clearly aspired to a kind of neoclassical grandeur, at the time a symbol of power and modernity. It has been pointed out that the development of the area around Grand Central Station gave rise to buildings that have, in their turn, marked the history of architecture. The Chrysler Building (New York, New York, United States; 1932) succeeded the Eiffel Tower as the tallest building in the world. In its style, it represented a shift away from neoclassicism and toward an art deco style related in part to the Chrysler automobiles of the time. Here, as in the case of the Eiffel Tower, there was a willful effort to incarnate a new, modern world of tall, shining towers. Just a few blocks away, and a few years later, the Seagram Building (New York, New York,

AEG Factory,
Berlin, Germany, 1910

Chrysler Building,
New York, New York, USA, 1930

United States; 1958) by Ludwig Mies van der Rohe sought a different kind of classicism, one that was inscribed in the modernist movement that rose from the ashes of Germany's Bauhaus and the presence in America of some of its leading lights, including Gropius and Mies.

Fallingwater, Rising Sun

Changes in architecture and its purposes have meant that throughout the twentieth century, an increasing number of essentially private projects began to attain the status of "great" buildings. Two residences published here, one of which was truly private and the other of which has always had a state function, illustrate the ways in which buildings can incarnate ideas. Fallingwater (Mill Run, Pennsylvania, United States; 1938), the Edgar J. Kaufmann House, built between 1936 and 1938, may be the most famous house of the twentieth century. The audacity of designing a house directly over a waterfall and using its massing and design to make the site into something more than it was naturally are hallmarks of Wright's style and genius. "I think nature should be spelled with a capital N," he said, "not because nature is God but because all that we can learn of God we will learn from the body of God, which we call nature." Though "organic" architecture has had a varied history, Wright's approach never consisted in mimicking nature, but rather in participating in it. As he writes in *The Future of Architecture*,

Seagram Building,
New York, New York, USA, 1958

> Change is the one immutable circumstance found in landscape. But the changes all speak or sing in unison of cosmic law, itself a nobler form of change. These cosmic laws are the physical laws of all man-built structures as well as the laws of the landscape. Man takes a positive hand in creation whenever he puts a building upon the earth beneath the sun. If he has a birthright at all, it must consist in this: that he, too, is no less a feature of the landscape than the rocks, trees, bears, or bees that nature to which he owes his being. Continuously nature shows him the science of her remarkable economy of structure in mineral and vegetable constructions to go with the unspoiled character everywhere apparent in her forms.

The significance of this approach may well be assimilated to a kind of revolutionary declaration of independence. Rather than existing merely to serve the whims of power, architecture could suddenly be viewed as a form of expression that has its own right to exist, somehow inscribed in the very laws of nature and life on earth.

Fallingwater,
Bear Run, Pennsylvania, USA, 1935

Oscar Niemeyer's Palace of the Dawn (Palácio da Alvorada, Brasília, Brazil; 1958) surely has a relationship to political power since it was conceived as, and is still, the official residence of the presidents of Brazil. Under construction even before Lúcio Costa's Pilot Plan for the new capital was accepted, the Palace of the Dawn faces the rising sun. Because of the unusual curving design of its supports, the building appears to float above the basins that mark its facade. The full symbolic import of the building is summed up in a quote from then newly elected president Juscelino Kubitschek: "From this central plateau, this vast loneliness that will soon become the center of national decisions, I look once more at the future of my country and foresee this dawn with an unshakeable faith in its great destiny." A lifelong Communist, Niemeyer felt like many others that Kubitschek would allow Brazil to attain its real promise as a new and shining example for its own population and the world at large. Though events would prove otherwise, the Palace of the Dawn still stands as testimony to the ways in which architecture can symbolize hope and renewal.

During the Renaissance, ecclesiastical architecture borrowed from classical tradition and verged toward the "dangerous" humanist thought that had become fashionable in Italy. In an interesting reversal of philosophy, many twentieth-century church buildings have tended more to look forward in their design. Though the affiliation is not always accepted as a fact, Oscar Niemeyer may well have had a considerable influence on the more lyrical production of Le Corbusier. In his autobiography, *The Curves of Time*, Niemeyer writes, "It was obvious that my architecture had influenced Le Corbusier's later projects, but this factor is only now being taken into account by critics of his work." He goes on to cite the memoirs of Amédée Ozenfant, the painter with whom Le Corbusier set out the doctrines of purism in the book *Après le cubisme* (1917). "After so many years of purist discipline and loyalty to the right angle," Ozenfant writes, "Le Corbusier caught wind of the premise of a new baroque from elsewhere, and he seems to have decided to leave aside the honest right-angle, which he tended to regard as his private domain for so long."

Modernity Forms Tradition

It is in his lyrical mode that Le Corbusier designed his most famous church, Notre Dame du Haut (Ronchamp, France; 1954). Built on a hilltop site in eastern France where Christian chapels have existed since the fourth century, it has a curved roof that appears almost to float above the walls. The thick southern wall of the church has irregular openings, almost denying the geometric rigor that Le Corbusier and other early-twentieth-century architects

Alvorada Palace,
Brasilia, Brazil, 1959

Notre Dame du Haut,
Ronchamp, France, 1954

had so warmly defended not many years before. As was often the case in the more distant past, a place of worship offers remarkable opportunities to a talented architect like Le Corbusier to break new ground, and to seek the spirituality that modernity often denies. With the light emerging from beneath its great roof, or from its patchwork of deep windows, Ronchamp represents a premonitory break with the architecture of industrial regularity that emerged from Germany early in the twentieth century and triumphed in the waves of post–World War II reconstruction. As was the case at Fallingwater, architecture here assumes its own identity, perhaps in service once again of the church, but somehow also succeeding in a quest to exist as a rightful and original form of artistic expression.

Although like art, great architecture sometimes takes time to be recognized, it is certain that two very different museum projects marked the end of the twentieth century. The first of these is the Grand Louvre (Paris, France; 1983–98), surely I. M. Peï's most significant work. Sometimes confused with the glass Pyramid (1989), which is in fact only the point of entry in the Cour Napoléon added by the Chinese American architect, the Grand Louvre project involved vast underground spaces and the reconstruction of the former Ministry of Finance offices in the Richelieu Wing of the palace. Part of the *Grands Travaux* willfully carried forward by French president François Mitterrand, the Louvre took on the historic heart of France, the place where its kings ruled, far more dense in its layers of history than Versailles could ever be.

Louvre Pyramid (Pyramide du Louvre), Grand Louvre, Paris, France, 1989–98

The Louvre actually sits at one end of the great perspective gardens stretching in the direction of the Tuileries and the present Champs-Élysées, gardens designed at the behest of Louis XIV by André Le Nôtre, who also worked at Versailles. Contrary to what many of its detractors have stated, the Louvre pyramid is in fact evidence of I. M. Peï's profound understanding of French tradition. He carefully studied the work of Le Nôtre and noted his masterful use of light, air, and water and geometric lines, such as the long axes laid out in Paris or at Versailles, for example. It is no accident that the glass surface of the pyramid reflects the Parisian sky, even as it defines the entrance area below, which is flooded with generous light. In this sense, and in its physical inscription within the walls of the historic Louvre palace, Peï's project does a great deal to reconnect contemporary architecture with the distant past, as his buildings often have. With visitor numbers approaching ten million persons per year, the Louvre is one of the most visited monuments in the world, a place where the present and the past come together, a place where art, too, is glorified. Despite the presence within the museum of Leonardo da Vinci's *Mona*

Lisa or the *Victory of Samothrace*, the real, living identity of the Louvre is defined and embodied by its architecture, both old and new.

The Crucible

A second museum project, which is significant for different reasons, is Frank Gehry's Guggenheim Bilbao (Bilbao, Spain; 1997). Like the movie stars whose names figure above the titles of their films, Gehry made himself into something of a rock star of the architecture world, claiming his right to design and build like an artist. Although it may be too early to judge its durability, Gehry's great titanium vessel, moored to the banks of the Nervión River in the heart of industrial Bilbao, is already considered one of the most important buildings of the late twentieth century. The architect Philip Johnson did not hesitate to call it "the greatest building of our time." It certainly brings to mind a great shining ship, anchored in the midst of a former port that had seen better days. It has also been an exceptional success story in terms of bringing an old industrial town back to life with culture. Crossed by a bridge, sitting at the water's edge, the Guggenheim Bilbao proclaims no real architectural style except for that of its designer. By drawing tourists to Bilbao it is somehow creating a new history for an old industrial town, incarnating the city in a newly fashioned avatar, one of modernity and cutting-edge esthetics.

Times have changed from an era when great buildings like the Gothic cathedrals might have taken centuries to erect. Now they go up in just a few years and may no longer seek to symbolize durability far greater than that of any human being. From being symbols of faith, power, and even the universe, great architecture has evolved into an expression of human inventiveness and perhaps, too, the personal triumph of Pritzker Prize winning architects. A complex such as the Louvre in Paris has demonstrated its durability over time and has even been modified, much as the great churches of the past evolved with their times. Pure creations such as the Guggenheim Bilbao will have to affront the judgment of many generations before their real status as witnesses to a place and time can be confirmed. Great architecture certainly stands witness to history, and in its most significant forms, it is the very crucible of change, societal development, art, culture, and history. In its most complete expression, architecture is what makes history possible. Architecture is not reserved for an elite in any sense; it is rather the substance from which country, culture, city, and identity are formed.

Philip Jodidio

October 30, 2012

Guggenheim Bilbao,
Bilbao, Spain, 1997

Discovering Architecture

537

Hagia Sophia

ISTANBUL, TURKEY

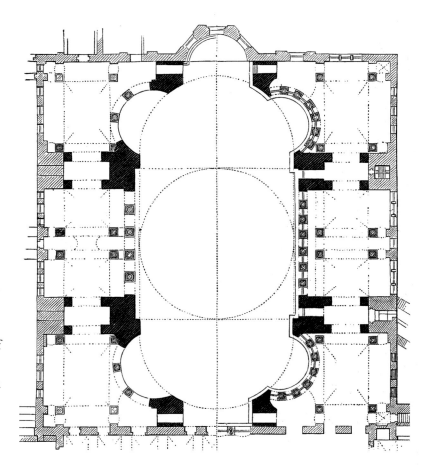

D ESIGNED BY the Byzantine Greek physicist Isidore of Miletus and the mathematician Anthemius of Tralles, Hagia Sophia is, in terms of both history and architecture, one of the most significant monuments in the world. Erected in just five years, it has served as an Eastern Orthodox cathedral, a Catholic cathedral, an imperial mosque, and finally, since 1935, a museum. Meaning "Holy Wisdom," Hagia Sophia, seat of the patriarch of Constantinople, was the largest cathedral in the world for almost one thousand years, with a rectangular plan measuring 253 by 233 feet (77 by 71 meters). Located on the site of two earlier churches, the basilica was built on the order of Justinian I, the Byzantine emperor from 527 to 565. It was inaugurated by the emperor and Eutychius, the ecumenical patriarch of Constantinople, on December 27, 537. Though it can be considered an ancient monument by any means, Hagia Sophia contains architectural elements that date from well before its construction in the sixth century, such as eight Corinthian columns brought from Baalbek on the order of the emperor.

The most significant aspect of the design is the dome, which collapsed in 558 subsequent to an earthquake. Its weight was carried by four arches resting on a series of pendentives and semidomes, which in turn transferred their weight to smaller semidomes and arcades. Deemed too flat, the original 102 foot (31 meter) diameter dome was rebuilt to be an additional 20.5 feet (6.25 meters) tall, allowing for the present interior height of 182 feet (55.6 meters) and relieving lateral pressure on the walls of the structure. Built with lighter materials, the new dome was designed by Isidorus the Younger, nephew of Isidore of Miletus. The basilica was rededicated by the patriarch on December 23, 562. Interior mosaics were completed under the rule of Justinian's successor Justin II (reigned 565–78), although the mosaics currently visible are of a later date.

Over time, the structure has been tried by earthquakes and fires, requiring many repairs to the vaults and domes. It was also the victim of ransacking at the time of the Fourth Crusade in 1204, which sealed the Great Schism between the Roman Catholic church and the Eastern Orthodox church. Until 1262 Hagia Sophia thus became a Catholic cathedral. Thereafter, the Byzantines returned the church to its original function, only to see it

again pillaged by the troops of the Ottoman sultan Mehmed II in 1453, marking the end of the Byzantine Empire. The young sultan immediately converted the church into an imperial mosque and renamed it Aya Sofya. A *mihrab*, signifying the direction of Mecca, was installed where the Christian altar had been, and in subsequent years minarets were erected around the church, and the celebrated mosaics were largely whitewashed.

Although its basic form is still that of the sixth-century building, Hagia Sophia was frequently modified. Because of earthquake risks, new buttresses were added to the exterior according to a design by the famous Ottoman architect Mimar Sinan during the rule of Sultan Selim II, a son of Suleiman the Magnificent who ruled from 1566 to 1577. Mimar Sinan further added minarets and a mausoleum that would be the tomb of the Ottoman princes. A golden crescent was placed on top of the dome, and Hagia Sophia remained a mosque until Mustafa Kemal Ataturk, founder of the Republic of Turkey, transformed it into a museum in 1935. A number of the figurative mosaics added to the church after the period of iconoclasm (726–843) were uncovered in the 1930s by an American group. The Historic Areas of Istanbul, including Hagia Sophia, were designated a UNESCO World Heritage Site in 1985.

Hagia Sofia
Istanbul, Turkey, 537

(RIGHT)
The walls buttressing the dome
were added after a partial collapse
in the sixteenth century.

691

Dome of the Rock

JERUSALEM, ISRAEL

IMAGINE A BUILDING that is at the heart of the holiest place of of both Judaism and Islam. The Dome of the Rock (Qubbat as-Sakhra) in Jerusalem was completed in 691 by the fifth Umayyad caliph, Abd al-Malik ibn Marwan (reigned 685–705), on the former site of Solomon's Temple, called the Holy of Holies. As such, it is the oldest extant monument of Islam. Not a mosque but a shrine for pilgrims, it covers a rock called the Foundation Stone, or the Pierced Stone, thought in Judaism to be the point of spiritual junction between heaven and earth, where the Ark of the Covenant containing the Ten Commandments was placed. It lies above a natural cave that is said to contain the Well of Souls, where Jews believe Abraham almost sacrificed Isaac. According to tradition, it is also the point of departure of the Prophet Mohammed on his "Night Journey" (*al-'Isrā' wal-Mi'rāj*) to heaven. Erected on a raised platform at the center of the Temple Mount (*al-Haram ash-Sharif*, or the Noble Sanctuary, in Arabic), the Dome of the Rock is located near Al Aqsa Mosque (first completed in 705), considered the third holiest place of Islam by Sunni Muslims.

Thought to be designed by the engineers Yazid Ibn Salam and Raja Ibn Haywah, the structure may well have been created to demonstrate the superiority of Islam over both Judaism and Christianity. In 1950, Shlomo Dov Goitein, then a professor at Hebrew University wrote,

> In a well-known passage of his *Book of Geography*, al-Maqdisi tells us how his uncle excused Abd al-Malik and Al-Walid I for spending so much good Muslims' money on buildings: They intended to remove the *fitna*, the "annoyance," constituted by the existence of the many fine buildings of worship of other religions. The very form of a rotunda, given to the Qubbat as-Sakhra, although it was foreign to Islam, was destined to rival the many Christian domes. The inscriptions decorating the interior clearly display a spirit of polemic against Christianity, while stressing at the same time the Quranic doctrine that Jesus Christ was a true prophet.

The celebrated dome of the shrine is approximately 66 feet (20.2 meters) in diameter and 67 feet (20.5 meters) tall, giving it almost exactly the same dimensions as the dome of the early-fourth-century Church of the Holy Sepulchre (335; rebuilt in 626). The wooden dome, clad in lead until the 1960s and in gold (leaf) since 1993, covers the Foundation Stone, which is at the center of the octagonal plan, said to be inspired by Byzantine structures used to house relics. It was on the orders of Suleiman the Magnificent, Ottoman emperor from 1520 to 1566, that the exterior of the structure was covered with colorful Iznik tiles. Marble, mosaics, and inscriptions from the Quran decorate the interior.

When the First Crusade arrived in Jerusalem in 1099, the Dome of the Rock was converted into the Templum Domini (Lord's Temple), because the Crusaders believed it was the actual temple built by Solomon. This conversion was made all the easier for the Crusaders because the structure's plan was not specifically related to any religion. When Jerusalem was recaptured in 1187 by the Ayyubid sultan Saladin (1137–1193), a golden crescent took the place of the cross on top of the dome. The Israeli administration has left the Dome of the Rock under the control of the Islamic Waqf Foundation, which administers the Temple Mount.

752

Todaiji Temple

NARA, JAPAN

MORE THAN thirteen hundred years ago, in 710, Nara became the imperial capital of Japan. Though it would retain this distinction for only seventy-four years, the city gave its name to the Nara period, which marked the permanent establishment of Buddhism in the country during the reign of Emperor Shōmu (724–749). The capital of Japan was transferred by Empress Gemmei (reigned 707–15) from Fujiwara to Nara, where a plan, based on Chinese cities such as Chang'an, was put in place. Palaces, Buddhist temples, Shinto shrines, public buildings, houses, and roads were laid out on an orthogonal grid with an area of approximately 6,200 acres (2,500 hectares). In 784 the imperial capital moved to Nagaoka for nine years, and then to Kyoto (Heian), where it remained until 1184.

The history of Todaiji Temple in Nara begins with a law and sculpture. In 743 Emperor Shōmu issued an edict asking the people to become directly involved in the construction of new Buddhist temples. To protect the country from disasters such as an outbreak of smallpox in 735, he also ordered the creation of a likeness of Buddha that would be called *Daibutsu* (Great Buddha), to be housed in a great wooden hall in Todaiji Temple, a name used as of 747. With an area of eight city blocks on each side, and twin seven-story pagodas that reached a height of 325 feet (99 meters), Todaiji became the largest temple of Nara and was given control of the nation's monasteries. Measuring nearly 50 feet (15 meters) tall, the Great Buddha was inaugurated in 752. Though he had officially abdicated in 749, Emperor Shōmu attended this "eye-opening ceremony," when an Indian priest painted in the eyes of the sculpture. The hall that houses the sculpture, the *Daibutsuden*, was rebuilt in 1709 at a scale approximately one third smaller than the original. But at 157 feet (48 meters) in height and a 187 by 164 foot (57 by 50 meter) footprint, it remains the largest old-wood

building in the world. The full compound of Todaiji was completed only in 798.

Both the Great Buddha and the temple itself were frequently damaged by fires and other events, burning to the ground in 1180, but they were then repaired or rebuilt. Some elements of the original temple, including the great pagodas, that were destroyed by earthquakes were never rebuilt. The most recent version of the Buddha sculpture dates from the end of the seventeenth century. This kind of continual reconstruction is typical of Japanese temples. Aside from its great hall, Todaiji Temple today includes seven other structures that are classified in Japan as national treasures. Only the Tegai Gate and the inner sanctuary of the Hokke-do (completed 745) remain amongst the original structures, although Shōsō-in, an eighth-century wooden storehouse for art and cultural treasures, was long under the care of the Todaiji (now controlled by the Imperial Household Agency). The main entrance to the temple is marked by the thirteenth-century Nandaimon, or Great Southern Gate. Todaiji is part of the Historic Monuments of Ancient Nara, which were added to the UNESCO World Heritage List in 1998.

972

Al-Azhar Mosque

CAIRO, EGYPT

IT IS RARE THAT a single monument embodies and symbolizes the history of a great city, and yet this is surely the case of Al-Azhar Mosque in Cairo. Though it occupies half of its original area, Al-Azhar remains a significant presence in modern Egypt, not least because of its university that counts no fewer than 64 faculties and 420,000 students.

The Fatimid dynasty (909–1171) controlled a good part of North Africa (now Algeria, Tunisia, and Egypt) as well as Sicily and Syria. The Fatimids were Ismaili Shia Muslims whose imam is said to descend from the daughter of the Prophet, Sayeda Fatima Al-Zahra'. The present Aga Khan is of this lineage, thus it is no coincidence that he created the 74 acre (30 hectare) Al Azhar Park near the mosque in 2005. Jawhar ibn Abdallah, who was called "al-Siqilli" (the Sicilian), the military leader of the Fatimids, reached the area he called al-Qahira (the Triumphant) in Egypt in 969, simultaneously founding the city of Cairo and its great new congregational mosque, Al-Azhar, whose name is in all likelihood derived from that of Zahra. The mosque was dedicated in 972, when Cairo officially became the capital of the Fatimid dynasty. A university associated with the mosque (*madrassa*) was also created. Long considered the leading university of the Arab world, it continues to operate today.

The original hypostyle structure had what is termed a "classical" design: "a *haram* (prayer hall) five bays deep, a central nave perpendicular to the *qibla* wall, a dome over the *mihrab* bay, three aisled arcades on the long sides of the *sahn* (courtyard) but none on the north side" (*The Mosque*, Thames & Hudson, London, 1994). The mosque has Corinthian marble columns dating from before the Islamic period. A wide transept leads to the *mihrab*. The *mihrab* signifies the direction of Mecca and thus the direction of prayer (*qibla*). Stucco panels and a window screen in the original *qibla* wall have survived, as have stucco decorations on the northeastern interior. An arcade on the fourth side of the courtyard was added in 1138, as were the oldest surviving

stained-glass windows in Egypt. The courtyard's white facade, decorated with rosettes and keel-arch panels, dates in part from the Fatimid period, while the very visible Qansah al-Ghuri and Qaytbay minarets were added by the Mamluks.

With the successive dynasties and changes of power in Egypt, the mosque had varying fortunes, losing its status as a Friday mosque under the Ayyubids, and regaining it under the Mamluk rulers. In 1996, Nasser Rabbat, a professor at the Massachusetts Institute of Technology, wrote, "The sequence of changes in al-Azhar's architecture reciprocates and reflects its rise to become the foremost institution of religious learning in Egypt and the concomitant political influence its denizens enjoyed among both the ruling classes and the general population. It also closely follows the fortune of the city of Cairo itself in its progress from capital of the self-consciously religious Fatimid dynasty to center of the aggressive and expansionist Mamluk military state, to provincial capital of the Ottoman Empire and finally to contemporary metropolis."

THE MINARET IS USED TO CALL
THE FAITHFUL TO PRAYER. THIS
ONE IS HIGHLY DECORATED WITH
THREE BALCONIES SUPPORTED ON
STALACTITE-LIKE VAULTING
NAMED *MUQARNAS*.

THIS DOME AND MINARET WERE
ERECTED IN 1339 TO MARK A STAND-
ALONE TOMB THAT WAS LATER
INTEGRATED INTO THE COMPLEX.

THE FOCAL POINT OF THE ARCADE
IS MARKED WITH SIX CORINTHIAN
COLUMNS SUPPORTING A POINTED
STILTED ARCH. THE COLUMNS ARE
REFERRED TO AS *SPOLIA*, OR REUSED
MATERIAL CREATED FOR AN EARLIER
BUILDING.

Al-Azhar Mosque
Cairo, Egypt, 972

(ABOVE)
View from the street of the gateway
to the mosque complex.

(RIGHT)
The marble paved interior courtyard of the mosque complex.

1250

Chartres Cathedral

CHARTRES, FRANCE

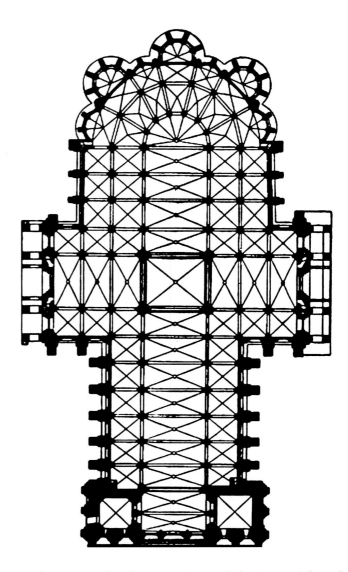

CONSTRUCTION OF THE Chartres Cathedral started in 1145, but it was rebuilt after a fire in 1194. The cathedral was consecrated in 1260, in the presence of King Louis IX of France. Inscribed on the UNESCO World Heritage List in 1979, "Chartres Cathedral marks the high point of French Gothic art. The vast nave, in pure ogival style, the porches adorned with fine sculptures from the middle of the 12th century, and the magnificent 12th- and 13th-century stained-glass windows, all in remarkable condition, combine to make it a masterpiece," according to the international organization. The term *ogival style* refers to the pointed arches used in the design.

Chartres is about 50 miles (80 kilometers) from Paris and was a Roman Catholic diocese as early as the third century, with at least four churches having been built on the same site as the present cathedral before the twelfth century. Characterized by flying buttresses and spires measuring 344.5 feet (105 meters, dating from approximately 1140) and 370.7 feet (113 meters, dating in its present form from the early 1500s), respectively, the structure is richly adorned with sculptures. The building is 427 feet (130 meters) long and 105 feet (32 meters) wide and 151 feet (46 meters) long. The nave is 121 feet (37 meters) high. The flying buttresses served in part to allow for the area of the 176 stained-glass windows to be larger, as did the pointed rib vaults. There are three large, round "rose" windows depicting the Last Judgment (west); the Virgin (north); and Christ (south). Approximately 150 of the original stained-glass windows survived the centuries, a higher proportion than in any other Gothic-period church. A few elements of the original stained glass survived the 1194 fire, but most of the windows now visible date from the period ranging between 1205 and 1240, a remarkable wealth of images and colors that fill the interior of the church with color and still impart the sense of awe intended by the original builders of the cathedral.

One unusual feature of the structure is its pavement labyrinth, a circular design 42.3 feet (12.9 meters) in diameter created in the thirteenth century in the midst of the floor of the nave. The Amiens Cathedral has a similar (though more octagonal) labyrinth, installed in 1288, while another example in Reims was removed in 1778 as a "symbol of superstition." Though the logic behind this labyrinth is still debated, the six-lobed rosette at its center was used to portray the nature of God in Sumerian, Babylonian, Jewish, and Roman art. Some studies link the labyrinth to the form of the cathedral's Last Judgment rose window. It has also been speculated that elements such as the ogive arches and rose windows present at Chartres and in Gothic architecture were inspired by early Islamic sources. Knowledge of these designs would have reached Europe through the Norman conquest of the emirate of Sicily (1085–91), the Crusades that began in 1096, as well as the Islamic presence in Spain that began in 711.

The cathedral has been one of the most frequented destinations for pilgrims in Europe since the twelfth century. Although work continued over the centuries, for example after the destruction of the lead-covered timber roof in 1836, the building has retained an authenticity that is exceptional for a structure of its age.

1150

Angkor Wat

SIEM REAP, CAMBODIA

ANGKOR, LOCATED IN the northern Cambodian province of Siem Reap, is one of the most significant archaeological sites in Southeast Asia. It covers approximately 154 square miles (400 square kilometers), including forested area. The ruins in this area, which was the capital of the Khmer Empire, date from the ninth to fifteenth century and include the Temple of Angkor Wat, built during the rule of Suryavarman II (1113–c.1150). The entire area, now called the Angkor Archeological Park, was inscribed on the UNESCO World Heritage List in 1992. Other well-known temples within the perimeter of the site, which was also remarkable because of its extensive irrigation system, include the Bayon, Preah Khan, and Ta Prohm, among dozens of others.

Angkor Wat, dedicated to Vishnu, was the largest Hindu temple in the world, and its form is felt to be a symbolic representation of Hindu cosmology. It was built as a state temple and, according to specialists, as a future mausoleum for the ruler. The central part of the design evokes Mount Meru, the home of demigods called *devas*. Its five towers represent the five peaks of the mountain. The mountain element of the temple is surrounded by three successive, richly sculpted rectangular galleries, and the entire temple is surrounded by walls 14.8 feet (4.5 meters) high and a moat that is 623.4 feet (190 meters) wide. The short dimensions of the compound are precisely aligned along a north–south axis. One clear reason for the extent of the walled area (202.6 acres, or 82 hectares), is that the now largely empty space was occupied by a city and a royal palace made of more perishable materials. The main material used for the temple is sandstone, with laterite employed for the outer walls. Considered a high point of Khmer architecture, the temple gave its name to the Angkor Wat style. Beginning at the end of the thirteenth century, Angkor Wat was used for Buddhist worship, which is still the case.

The inner wall carvings of Angkor Wat represent Apsara at least two thousand times. Apsara is the beautiful, supernatural female spirit of the water and clouds in both Hindu and Buddhist belief, usually depicted with bare breasts. The exterior walls at the lowest levels have low-relief sculptures figuring Hindu mythology, mixed with the wars led by Suryavarman II, such as his march against the Cham, who came from the east. Long abandoned, the complex of Angkor Wat was brought to world attention in 1860 by the French explorer Henri Mouhot (1826–1861), although other Europeans, such as the Portuguese trader Diogo do Couto (1542–1616) and the Capuchin friar Antonio da Madalena, wrote of their visits to the site in the sixteenth century. Speaking of Angkor Wat, Mouhot wrote, "One of these temples—a rival to that of Solomon, and erected by some ancient Michelangelo—might take an honorable place beside our most beautiful buildings. It is grander than anything left to us by Greece or Rome." Following Mouhot's visit, the first of many restoration schemes was undertaken, continuing to this day with the help of France, India, or Germany.

THE SANDSTONE TOWER REPRESENTS ONE
OF THE FIVE PEAKS OF MOUNT MERU, THE
HOME OF THE DEMIGODS CALLED *DEVAS*.

THE SITE IS DECORATED WITH
THOUSANDS OF CARVED IMAGES OF
ASPARA, THE FEMALE SPIRIT OF WATER
AND CLOUDS IN BOTH THE HINDU AND
BUDDHIST MYTHOLOGIES.

1280–1350

Piazza del Campo

SIENA, ITALY

THE PIAZZA DEL CAMPO is the main public space of the historic center of Siena in Tuscany. The unusual semi circular shell shape of the square is formed by the Palazzo Pubblico, built between 1297 and 1308 on the lower side, and a series of private palaces of the same height along the upper edge (*palazzi signorili*). The piazza developed from the market that existed on the site prior to the thirteenth century, at the juncture of three earlier towns (and of three hills), with eleven streets radiating from the square. The relative uniformity of the architecture still seen today is no accident—city ordinances regulated the dimensions of each house and the twin or triple arched form of the windows. A church built on the square dedicated to saints Peter and Paul was demolished because it did not respect the regulations, a measure of the strictness of the rules. Given the irregularity of the natural terrain, the unity achieved by this square makes it one of the great examples of urbanism in the world. The sloping, enclosing form of the square also differentiates it from many flatter urban spaces.

The period when the Campo developed also corresponds to the presence of such great artists as Duccio di Buoninsegna (1260–1318), Simone Martini (1284–1344), and Ambrogio Lorenzetti (1319–48), who decorated the Hall of the Nine in the Palazzo Pubblico. Frescos by Martini, such as the *Equestrian Portrait of Guidoriccio da Fogliano*, are located in the Sala del Mappamondo of the Palazzo Pubblico. Other elements were added to the square over time, such as the 289 foot (88 meter) high Torre del Mangia, adjoining the Palazzo Pubblico, which was built between 1328 and 1348. To the northwest, the Fonte Gaia (Fountain of Joy), with sculptures originally by Jacopo della Quercia, was completed in 1419, when it replaced a fourteenth-century fountain as part of a city water system. Fragments of the original are preserved in the Palazzo Pubblico.

The Campo itself was paved between 1327 and 1349 under the auspices of the Council of Nine (Governo dei Nove), who ruled Siena from 1287 to 1355. The square is paved in unusual "knife"-shaped bricks symbolically divided into nine sections by lines of travertine marble. These lines converge toward the Palazzo Pubblico as the logical center of power in Siena. The

fishbone pattern employed for the bricks may recall the Roman technique in the use of this paving material.

The Piazza del Campo was long the location of public games in the style of jousting and then bullfighting. After 1590, when bullfighting was outlawed, the Campo became the location for horse races (*Palio di Siena*) that pit the areas of the city against one another each year on July 2 and August 16, a tradition that continues to attract tourists.

The historic center of Siena, surrounded by nearly four and a half miles (7 kilometers) of ramparts dating from the fourteenth to the sixteenth century, was inscribed on the UNESCO World Heritage List in 1995. As the organization states, "The whole city of Siena, built around the Piazza del Campo, was devised as a work of art that blends into the surrounding landscape."

Piazza del Campo
Siena, Italy, 1280–1350

(ABOVE)
The *palio*, or horserace, takes
place in the *campo* yearly on
July 2 and August 16.

(RIGHT)
The *campo* fans out from the
Palazzo Pubblico, creating one
of the most spectacular piazzas
in Italy.

CA. 1424

Doge's Palace

VENICE, ITALY

THE MANY TOURISTS who come to Venice inevitably notice the rather unexpected architecture of the Doge's Palace (Palazzo Ducale), with its pink Verona marble facade and long row of arches facing the lagoon and St. Mark's Square. While the arch design brings to mind the Gothic period, there is something decidedly oriental or perhaps Byzantine about this building, set close to the even more Byzantine Basilica of St. Mark, whose present form dates from 1063. The object of close study and extensive commentary over time, the Doge's Palace was called "the central building of the world" by the English critic John Ruskin (1819–1900).

As is often the case of such ancient, centrally placed structures, the Doge's Palace was not the first building to occupy its site. Records indicate that a palace for the doge was built in wood on the same location in 814. It burned during a revolt against Doge Pietro IV Candiano in 976 and was rebuilt under the rule of the Doge Sebastiano Ziani (1172–78), but a newer structure was created starting in 1340. Its completion was undertaken in 1424, with the extension of two identical facades facing the broad stone quay at the waterside (the *Molo*) and the Piazzetta San Marco, respectively. Construction of the main gateway to the palace, the Porto della Carta, was undertaken in 1438 with a design by Giovanni and Bartolomeo Buon. The public entrance today is through the Porta del Frumento, approached through the colonnade under the waterfront facade. Another fire in 1483 damaged the doge's residence, leading to reconstruction of the eastern wing in a Renaissance style, apparently by the architect and sculptor Antonio Rizzo (1430–1499). Fires again ravaged the palace in 1547 and 1577. The latter destroyed works by such artists as Il Pisanello, Titian, Giovanni Bellini, and Gentile da Fabriano. Andrea Palladio proposed a neoclassical design, but it was decided to rebuild the palace in a Gothic form. Paintings by Paolo Veronese and Tintoretto, which still exist, became part of the interior decor.

The celebrated Bridge of Sighs (Ponte dei Sospiri), designed by Antoni Contino, was completed in 1614 to link the palace to new prisons located on the opposite side of the Rio di Palazzo.

In his celebrated work *The Stones of Venice*, Ruskin equates the complex history of the Doge's Palace with that of Venice itself. He writes, "The Ducal Palace of Venice contains the three elements in exactly equal proportions—the Roman, Lombard, and Arab. It is the central building of the world." He also wrote of "the building which at once consummates and embodies the entire system of the Gothic architecture of Venice—the Ducal Palace." Seat of power of the Republic of Venice, the palace has been restored continually but has retained much of its unique layering of different periods of history. Formed in a Byzantine style that Ruskin associates with the foundation of the Venetian republic, it was replaced by the Gothic palace in the early fourteenth century, which coincided with the emergence of aristocratic rule. For Ruskin, the Gothic ducal palace was "the Parthenon of Venice."

1461

Pazzi Chapel

FLORENCE, ITALY

FILIPPO BRUNELLESCHI (1377–1446) was one of the leading architects and engineers of the Italian Renaissance. He is responsible not only for the design of the dome of the Florence Cathedral (1446–61), but also for the discovery of the geometric method of perspective (1461). Located in the cloister of the Basilica of Santa Croce in Florence (completed in 1442), the Pazzi Chapel, commissioned in 1429 by Andrea Pazzi, was built beginning in 1441. Brunelleschi also worked on the Basilica of San Lorenzo in Florence at the behest of the Medici family. Like the Pazzi Chapel, San Lorenzo was not completed in its substance until after the architect's death, in 1461. It has been suggested that although the basic design of the chapel was indeed by Brunelleschi, Giuliano da Maiano or Michelozzo di Bortalommeo may have been responsible for its construction, which commenced only near the end of Brunelleschi's life. It has been underlined that this question of the "paternity" of one of the great monuments of the Italian Renaissance also is indicative of the rise of architects and artists who were known as individuals. Earlier ecclesiastical architecture is most often anonymous in its conception. Simple in its geometry and decoration, it might be said that the Pazzi Chapel is in a sense the prototypical "modern" building, the work of a "genius," even if we are not quite sure which one.

The same kind of mathematical approach, consisting of geometric formulas, used in the discovery of perspective was employed by the architect for the design of the Pazzi Chapel. Its plan and section are made up of a central domed space flanked on two sides by barrel-vaulted side bays and on the third by a small domed recess set behind an arch. The circle and the rectangle or square are the basic forms employed. The structure was designed as a chapter house (meeting room or teaching space for monks), with a chapel behind the altar intended for

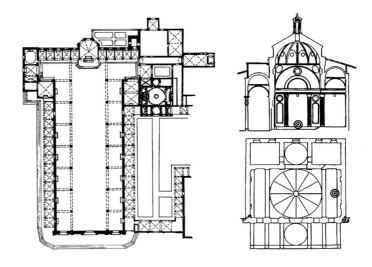

the burial of members of the Pazzi family. Built after the architect's death, a portico with an interior dome decorated by Luca della Robbia greets visitors, admitting some light into the interior, where a twelve-ribbed hemispherical dome covers the space. A circular opening at the top of the dome allows natural light to enter the space, as does a series of twelve *oculi* around the base of the dome. The exterior of the chapel was never finished, apparently because Brunelleschi left no precise instructions. White plaster and gray *pietra serena* were used for the interior design. Enameled terracotta roundels representing the apostles by Luca della Robbia are placed around the interior space. It is speculated that the four roundels representing the evangelists that are located at the base of the dome may have been designed by Brunelleschi or Donatello and then glazed in the della Robbia workshop. A 2009 restoration of the interior of the cupola above the altar revealed details of a fresco by an unknown artist that represents mythical figures of constellations in the sky of Florence on July 4, 1442.

1420/70

Santa Maria Novella

FLORENCE, ITALY

SANTA MARIA NOVELLA, a Dominican church, was built beginning in 1246 on the site of the ninth-century oratory of Santa Maria delle Vigne, in Florence. The design of the structure is attributed to a number of friars, beginning with the architect monks Fra Ristoro da Campi and Fra Sisto Fiorentino. As is often the case for such significant monuments, Santa Maria Novella is made up of various additions and extensive remodeling. The result is that the church is a repository of some of the greatest works of Renaissance architecture and art. Even its renovations were carried out by such famous artists as Giuliano da Sangallo (Gondi Chapel, 1501). Amongst its architectural elements are a pointed bell tower in Romanesque-Gothic style (1330), the so-called Spanish Chapel (1350–55) and a refectory added at about the same time. Although the church was consecrated in 1420, one of its most remarkable additions was begun only about 1456. The white and black marble facade of the church, which now faces the Unità d'Italia Square, completed in 1470, is the work of the architect and writer Leon Battista Alberti (1404–1472). Alberti, like the older Brunelleschi, studied the mathematical aspects of perspective and was known for many other accomplishments aside from his architectural work.

The commission for the facade of the church was made by the wool merchant and banker Giovanni di Paolo Rucellai (1403–81), for whom Alberti had already designed the facade of the Palazzo Rucellai on the Via della Vigna Nuova in Florence (1446–51, probably executed by Bernardo Rossellino). Because work on the facade of Santa Maria Novella had begun in 1300, Alberti sought to harmonize existing medieval elements with his own design, which was based on harmonic proportions related to those employed in music. Squares have half-size squares inscribed in them and so on, with a constant proportion of one to two. Triangles and circles are also employed in the same spirit.

The church contains such masterpieces as a crucifix by Giotto (1288–89), placed at the center of the nave; the *Trinità* by Masaccio (1425–27); crucifixes by Giambologna and Brunelleschi; and frescos by Domenico Ghirlandaio, a *Nativity* by Sandro Botticelli, and the Rucellai Madonna by Duccio di Buoninsegna (commissioned in 1285, now in the Uffizi Gallery). The frescoes in the cloisters are the work of Paolo Uccello and the Florentine school (13th–15th centuries).

Masaccio's work employs a kind of trompe-l'oeil perspective that is thought to have been created for its precise location in the basilica, giving an illusion of "real" architectural space. In his celebrated work *Lives of the Most Excellent Painters, Sculptors and Architects* (enlarged version, 1568), Giorgio Vasari wrote of "a barrel vault drawn in perspective, and divided into squares with rosettes which diminish and are foreshortened so well that there seems to be a hole in the wall." Curiously, when he undertook the extensive renovation of Santa Maria Novella, also in 1568, Vasari chose to place an altar and screen in front of Masaccio's work, which was rediscovered only on the occasion of new renovation work in 1860. In a less enlightened mode, the church is also known as the place where the Dominican Tommaso Caccini denounced the nature of the work of Galileo Galilei, leading to the scientist's trials for heresy.

Santa Maria Novella
Florence, Italy, 1420/1470

(ABOVE)
Page 72 above: The main altar
includes a bronze Cruxifix by
Giambologna and frescoes by
Domenico Ghirlandaio.

(RIGHT)
The irregularly shaped piazza
includes two obelisks that served
as turning posts for the annual
Palio dei Cocchi that was held
until the mid-nineteenth century.

1420

Forbidden City

BEIJING, CHINA

THE FORBIDDEN CITY was the seat of Chinese power from 1416 to 1911, fully embodying Chinese palace architecture. With its main Meridian Gate on the south, the palace has an axial design and symmetric plan with successive courtyards, covering an area of more than 178 acres (72 hectares). The overall plan is rectangular, measuring 3,153 feet (961 meters) from north to south and 2,470 feet (753 meters) from east to west, and the whole is surrounded by a 25.9 foot (7.9 meter) high wall and a moat, with gates in each of the four cardinal directions. Beyond the Meridian Gate, farther to the south, the Tiananmen Gate (Gate of Heavenly Peace), built in 1465 replacing an earlier structure, opens into Tiananmen Square, the third largest city square in the world.

Under the orders of Emperor Zhu Di (also called the Yongle Emperor; 1360–1424), construction of the imperial palace began in 1407 and was completed in 1420. The site chosen was part of the earlier Yuan dynasty imperial city, which had been demolished in 1369 on the order of the Hongwu Emperor (1328–1398), who was the father of Zhu Di. Stone was quarried in Fangshan, nearly 24 miles (38 kilometers) distant, and enormous trees were cut in Sichuan province (932 miles, or 1,500 kilometers, away) for the main buildings, with more than one hundred thousand artisans and a million workers participating in the construction. A total of fourteen Ming dynasty emperors, followed by ten during the Qing dynasty, ruled from the Forbidden City.

The Forbidden City contains no fewer than 980 buildings and nearly ten thousand rooms, with the most significant structures placed in the center on a north–south axis. The actual axis is slightly more than two degrees removed from north–south alignment, perhaps a reminiscence of an earlier Yuan dynasty plan that pointed in the direction of Xanadu (Shangdu, the summer capital of Kublai Khan). In the Forbidden City, the Hall of Supreme Harmony, the Hall of Central Harmony, and the Hall of Preserving Harmony form the outer palace where the emperor exercised power. The Hall of Heavenly Purity, the Hall of Union, and the Hall of Earthly Tranquility make up the inner palace where the imperial family lived. The 98.4 foot (30 meter) high Hall of Supreme Harmony, where the emperor held court

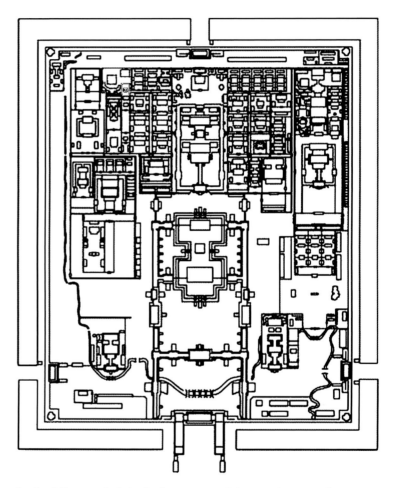

in the Ming period, is the largest surviving ancient wood structure in China. Taoist and Buddhist temples or chambers also dot the complex. The design of the Forbidden City is marked by such landscape features as the Golden Water River, located inside the Meridian Gate and in front of the Gate of Supreme Harmony. This artificial river is crossed by bridges representing the five virtues identified by Confucius: benevolence, righteousness, rites, intelligence, and fidelity.

Converted into the Palace Museum in 1925, the complex is considered to be one of the largest and best-preserved examples of wooden palace architecture in the world. Parts of the original collections of the Forbidden City were transferred in the late 1940s to the National Palace Museum in Taipei. The Forbidden City was added to the UNESCO World Heritage List in 1987.

1502–10

Tempietto

SAN PIETRO IN MONTORIO, ROME, ITALY

SUBSEQUENT TO THE FLIGHT of his patron Ludovico Sforza during the French invasion of Milan in 1499, the architect Donato Bramante (1444–1514) went to Rome, where he was commissioned in 1502 by Ferdinand of Aragon and Isabella of Castile to build a small structure called the Tempietto in the cloister of the Church of San Pietro in Montorio. The location was thought to be the site of the crucifixion of St. Peter. The church was built on the site of an earlier church on the Janiculum (Gianicolo) hill. The centrally planned, circular Tempietto is related in its conception to Roman and early Christian martyria, monuments erected as memorials or to commemorate events of particular significance. During the period of the realization of the Tempietto, Bramante would also design the Cortile del Belvedere (Belvedere Courtyard) in the Vatican as a sculpture court for antique works for Pope Julius II. He had a great interest in Roman or Greek civilization, and the celebrated sculptures of *Laocoön and His Sons* and the *Apollo Belvedere* were exhibited in the courtyard. He also created a design for St. Peter's Basilica (1505).

It has been suggested that the Tempietto represents an effort to reconcile Christian doctrine with the humanist influences that are reflected in the taste for antique art evident in the Belvedere Courtyard. It was in approximately 1490 that Leonardo da Vinci made his celebrated drawing of a figure inscribed in a circle, together with an Italian translation of the relevant text by Vitruvius (80–15 B.C.), which posits that a well-proportioned man fits, with arms and legs extended, into perfect geometric forms— the circle and square. More precisely, Vitruvius wrote, "without symmetry and proportion no temple can have a regular plan; that is, it must have an exact proportion worked out after the fashion of the limbs of the finely shaped human body." Both Leonardo, who imagined centrally planned and domed churches, and Bramante worked for Ludovico Sforza. It has further been speculated that during a visit to Rome in 1504, the two men may have discussed the Tempietto. In his *Four Books of Architecture* (1570), Andrea Palladio wrote, "Since Bramante was the first to make known that good and beautiful architecture which had been hidden from the times of the ancients until now; I thought it

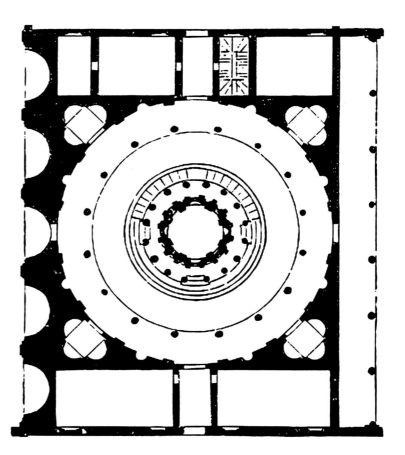

reasonable that his work should be placed amongst those of the ancients." Noting the extreme simplicity of the design, Palladio further wrote, "The columns are granite, the bases and capitals marble, and all the rest is travertine."

According to a period document, the architect's intention was to create a square colonnaded courtyard around the Tempietto, whose diameter is just 15 feet (4.6 meters). Surrounded by sober Tuscan Doric columns, the structure is covered by a semicircular dome. An underground chamber theoretically marks the location of the martyrdom of St. Peter. Aside from its evident simplicity, the Tempietto shares another characteristic with certain works of more modern architecture. It is hardly large enough to serve a specific purpose other than commemoration, surely more like a tomb than a chapel, and yet it is also so voluntarily artistic that it might also be likened to a sculpture.

1534

Palazzo del Te

MANTUA, ITALY

THE ARTIST Giulio Romano was born, as his artist's name implies, in Rome between 1492 and 1499 and died in Mantua in 1546. A painter and architect, he is considered an heir to Raphael and is certainly one of the creators of Mannerism in Italy. He moved from Rome to Mantua in 1524 and started work the following year on his most significant realization, the Palazzo del Te, for Federico II Gonzaga, Duke of Mantua (1500–1540). The basic structure was completed in just eighteen months, but the decoration took nearly ten years. Working with pupils and local artists, Giulio Romano built and entirely decorated the palace, which is located on the southern outskirts of the city, aligned with its central axis. The basic plan is constituted of a square form that is developed around a central courtyard that was to have been occupied by a labyrinth. The square courtyard measures 145 feet (44.2 meters) on each side. As Giorgio Vasari describes the genesis of this project, the duke brought Giulio Romano to the island of Te, just outside the city walls, and asked him to restructure existing stables as a palace for recreation and leisure. The Palazzo del Te was inspired by the Roman precedent of the *villa suburbana*. Externally, its rusticated appearance does not necessarily announce the painted turmoil within. This is a remarkable example of the fusion of art and architecture in a single building.

The principal rooms of the Palazzo del Te are dedicated to myth but also to the horses of the Gonzaga. The Sala di Psiche is decorated with frescoes representing the story of Cupid and Psyche, as recounted in the *Metamorphoses* of Apuleius (125–180). The Sala dei Cavalli has lifesize portraits of Gonzaga horses and trompe-l'oeil classical architecture in the Corinthian order. Decorated before the full completion of the palazzo, the Sala dei Cavalli was where the duke received the Holy Roman Emperor Charles V during his visit to Mantua in 1530. The most famous space of the interior of the Palazzo del Te is the Sala dei Giganti. It features a floor-to-ceiling representation of the fall of

the giants as described in the *Metamorphoses* by the Roman poet Ovid (43 B.C.–A.D. 17). The Sala dei Giganti was completed in 1534 with the active participation of the painter Rinaldo Mantovano. In his *Lives of the Artists*, Giorgio Vasari wrote of this room, "Wherefore let no one ever think to see any work of the brush more horrible and terrifying, or more natural than this one; and whoever enters that room and sees the windows, doors, and other suchlike things all awry and, as it were, on the point of falling, and the mountains and buildings hurtling down, cannot but fear that everything will fall upon him, and, above all, as he sees the Gods in the Heaven rushing, some here, some there, and all in flight." Three centuries later, less enchanted, Charles Dickens wrote of the Sala dei Giganti in his *Pictures from Italy* (1846): "The figures are immensely large, and exaggerated to the utmost pitch of uncouthness; the coloring is harsh and disagreeable; and the whole effect more like (I should imagine) a violent rush of blood to the head of the spectator, than any real picture set before him by the hand of the artist."

Palazzo del Te
Mantua, Italy, 1534

The continuous fresco connecting walls and vaulted ceiling depicts the Fall of the Giants from Ovid's *Metamorphoses*.

1571

Villa Almerico Capra, La Rotonda

VICENZA, ITALY

IN *I QUATTRO LIBRI DELL'ARCHITETTURA* (The Four Books of Architecture, 1570), the architect Andrea Palladio (1508–1580) writes,

> The site is one of the most pleasing and delightful that one could find because it is on top of a small hill which is easy to ascend; on one side it is bathed by the Bacchiglione, a navigable river, and on the other is surrounded by other pleasant hills which resemble a vast theater and are completely cultivated and abound with wonderful fruit and excellent vines; so, because it enjoys the most beautiful vistas on every side, some of which are restricted, others more extensive, and yet others which end at the horizon . . .

Palladio, one of the most influential architects in history, refers in this text to the Villa Almerico Capra, also called the Villa Rotonda, built just outside Vicenza for Paolo Almerico (1514–1589), a priest and poet. The house was built quickly by the standards of the time (1567–71). The Villa Rotonda, as its name implies, has a central round hall and a dome, which is inscribed in the square form of the house itself, with four porticos with Ionic-style columns. The plan might be considered unusual because it is entirely symmetrical, though the steps that descend into the natural setting do have variations in their retaining walls and embankments. Palladio was greatly influenced by classical architecture and Vitruvius, and he sought here to translate something of the inspiration of ecclesiastical architecture to the domain of private villas. This structure is thus in a sense a sort of temple, located in fields that are not defined as closed gardens.

The intention of the architect was to provide sunlight and views of the landscape to every room. Sunlight is the reason that the plan is rotated forty-five degrees to the south, giving more rooms direct natural light. The architecture is ornamented with sculptures thought to be by Lorenzo Rubini and Giambattista Albanese. Frescoes inside the dome were a later addition, commissioned by Odorico Capra. The Capra family bought the villa

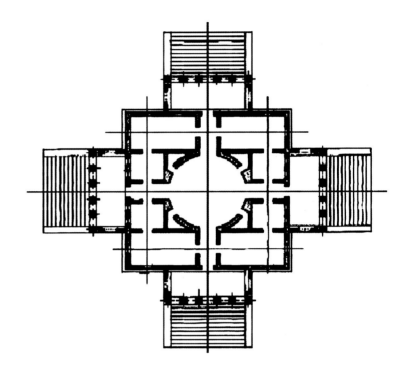

in 1591 and called on the Venetian architect Vincenzo Scamozzi to oversee work on the structure, which included a design for the central dome that was lower than the one originally planned by Palladio. A half elevation and half section of the house showing the architect's original intention is published in Palladio's *Quattro libri*. Scamozzi's dome is modeled after that of the Pantheon in Rome, and his work was finished in 1606. The French artist Louis Dorigny painted frescoes in the hall and corridors at the beginning of the eighteenth century.

Now more encumbered by neighboring farm structures than it was at the time of its construction, the Villa Rotonda served as a model for the noble country homes of England in the eighteenth century, as evidenced by Mereworth (Colen Campbell, Kent; 1722) or Chiswick House (Lord Burlington, Middlesex; 1725). The Villa Rotonda was placed on the UNESCO World Heritage List in 1994. It has been fully open to the public since 1986.

After Palladio's death, Scamozzi completed the villa and changed the bold central dome to a lower, more Roman-inspired form.

Palladio mistakenly believed that the temple developed from the Roman house. His use of the temple portico to frame entrances became one of the most often employed elements in Western architecture.

Palladio studied surviving Roman buildings and used this knowledge to create this finely detailed Ionic column and entablature.

CA. 1500

Ryoan-ji

KYOTO, JAPAN

THE *KARESANSUI*, or Japanese dry landscape garden (also called "withered landscapes"), is in the strictest sense an artificial creation. Having no specific purpose other than contemplation, it may not be considered a work of architecture, and yet such gardens form an integral part of many temples. The garden at Ryoan-ji in Kyoto, thought to have been built in the late 1400s by the artist Soami (1480?–1525), is the most famous of these. The garden consists of raked gravel and fifteen moss-covered stones, placed so that from any angle only fourteen can be seen at once. It is said that only when one attains spiritual enlightenment as a result of deep Zen meditation is it possible to see the last, invisible stone with the mind's eye. Although the temple structures that surround the garden date from the late eighteenth century, Ryoan-ji is also made up of surrounding walls and the long platform from which visitors can view the garden. The garden is an integral part of the architecture and vice versa. Numerous interpretations have been given to explain the enduring popularity and "meaning" of Ryoan-ji, though none can be conclusive.

The writer Günter Nitschke has suggested that the garden is more about emptiness or the void than it is a figurative construct, as others have claimed. The representation of the void encourages visitors to look within. More recently a study by neuroscientists has suggested that there may well be an underlying pattern in Ryoan-ji—a subliminal tree. In these terms, in the dry rocks and gravel of Ryoan-ji, a tree grows, one that is perceived only by the mind's eye. It is also said that in Buddhism, the number fifteen signifies wholeness or completeness. In the rock garden, if a person can see all fifteen stones, it means that they have attained enlightenment.

The Zen Buddhist temple of Ryoan-ji (the Temple of the Dragon at Peace) was founded at the death of the warlord Katsumoto Hosokawa (1430–1473), but built only in the final years of the fifteenth century. The temple and probably the garden were built by his son Matsumoto Hosokawa, although some historians believe the garden may have been created much later

(17th century). The temple burned in 1797. It was restored, and a clay wall behind it and a viewing platform in front were created. The temple is also known as the site of the tombs of seven early emperors of Japan, who were members of the Hosokawa clan.

Ryoan-ji is affiliated with the Rinzai branch of Zen Buddhism brought to Japan from China by the monk Myoan Eisai (1141–1215). Rinzai places an emphasis on *kensho*, a word that signifies "seeing nature," and thus perceiving the self. Ideally, this experience implies the lack of distinction between the seer and the thing seen. It is believed that all phenomena come into being because of conditions created by other phenomena, and thus have not existence of their own. The extreme simplicity of the Ryoan-ji garden together with its enduring mystery make it a high point of Japanese culture, no matter what its date of creation.

ONE OF THE 15 STONES IN THE GARDEN
THAT IS A FOCUS OF CONTEMPLATION.
THE LIMITED GARDEN ELEMENTS CONVEY
APPRECIATION FOR UNDERSTATEMENT
AND SIMPLICITY.

THE ENCLOSING WALL CONVEYS A
NATURAL APPEARANCE. MADE OF CLAY
WITH RANDOM STAINS OF BROWN AND
ORANGE, IT IS PROTECTED BY A ROOF
OF BARK, RESTORED TO THIS ORIGINAL
MATERIAL IN 1977.

THE ZEN GARDEN USES LIMITED
MATERIALS. THE PRINCIPAL ONE
IS ROUGH SAND RAKED DAILY IN
CAREFUL PATTERNS BY THE MONKS.

1572–85

Fatehpur Sikri Palace

FATEHPUR SIKRI, INDIA

FATEHPUR SIKRI is a palace complex built by the third Mughal emperor, Jalal'ud-Din Muhammad Akbar (1542–1605). The palace is located on a 131 foot (40 meter) high hill and near an artificial lake. The emperor first built a small palace on the site (1569), apparently before deciding to make it his capital or administrative center. Fatehpur Sikri (City of Victory) is located near the old city of Sikri on the road between the cities of Agra, which is 24.85 miles (40 kilometers) distant, and Ajmer. The main structures aligned in a north–south direction were built between 1572 and 1575, with numerous corridors added in the period 1575–85. The palace area is protected on three sides by a wall 3.73 miles (6 kilometers) long, which has towers and seven gates. The nature of the construction suggests that the goal was not to create a fort, but rather to mark the limits of the palace. The layout of the complex is believed to have influenced the evolution of Indian town planning, in particular in Old Delhi.

In 1585, an English traveler named Ralph Fitch wrote that the palace complex and city around it were "considerably larger than London and more populous." Although this appreciation might seem somewhat exaggerated, it nonetheless indicates the presence of a large population about which relatively little is known. In 1585, the emperor moved the court to Lahore, abandoning Fatehpur Sikri in the process. The complex served as the Mughal capital again in 1619, but only for a period of three months. Archeological work on the site that constitutes the largest preserved complex of Mughal architecture was undertaken beginning in 1892. Only the areas where the major buildings are located have been carefully studied, however.

The upper level of the complex is occupied by the spacious Great Mosque (Jama Masjid), facing Mecca and large enough to accommodate ten thousand worshippers. It covers an area of 541 by 436 feet (165 by 133 meters). The white marble tomb of the Sufi saint Salim Chishti (1478–1572) is located in the courtyard. The site of Fatehpur Sikri was the place of birth of the future Emperor Jahangir (1569–1627), a son of Akbar, that had been predicted by Salim Chisti.

The palace is located on two lower platforms. The middle level was reserved for the residences of the emperor, whereas the bottom platform included public and semipublic structures. In the complex that originally included sixty buildings, forty still exist, but of these only thirteen are fully documented in terms of their original function. What is clear is that the designers of Fatehpur Sikri relied on a geometric scheme based in part on the golden section. The entire plan of the complex is probably organized on the basis of a 32-inch (81.28-centimeter) grid. The main construction material was red sandstone, with standard dimensions used for the locally quarried stone, which was modified on site as required. Despite the apparent rigor of the design, the forms and plans employed are a mixture of Hindu, Persian, and Indo-Muslim inspiration, in effect creating a new Mughal style. Fatehpur Sikri was inscribed on the UNESCO World Heritage List in 1986.

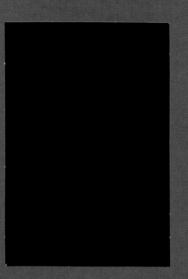

WHITE MARBLE SERPENTINE BRACKETS SUPPORT THE OVERHANGING ROOF OF THE TOMB OF THE SUFI SAINT SALIM CHISHTI.

THE TWO-STORY GATEWAY ARCH SURROUNDED BY RECTANGULAR FRAME IS A COMMON FEATURE IN ISLAMIC ARCHITECTURE. IN INDIA IT IS TERMED A *PISHTAQ*.

CLASSICAL COLUMNS HAVE THREE MAJOR DIVISIONS: BASE, SHAFT, AND CAPITAL. THIS COLUMN HAS THE SAME DIVISIONS BUT IS FAR MORE ORNATE THAN COLUMNS IN THE WESTERN WORLD.

Fatehpur Sikri Palace
Fatehpur Sikri, India, 1572–85

(ABOVE)
Geometric openings in a
screen of carved stone.

(RIGHT)
The Tomb of Salim Chishti
is located in the courtyard
of the Jama Masjid Mosque,
Fatehpur Sikri.

220 B.C.–A.D. 1644

Great Wall

CHINA

PERHAPS NO SINGLE structure of any kind on earth has been so continuously expanded and maintained as the Great Wall. With a total length of 12,427 miles (20,000 kilometers), it is by far the longest man-made structure. Long said to be visible even from the moon, it appears that, because of its average width and the similar color of the surrounding landscape, the Great Wall cannot be seen even from earth's orbit without the aid of binoculars or a telescope. This, of course, by no means diminishes the scale of the architectural achievement that it represents.

The Great Wall begins in Shanhaiguan, in Hebei province, and ends in Jiayuguan, in Gansu province, at its western end. Those who have visited the parts of the wall that are open to the public, in the hills near Beijing at Badaling, realize to what extent this architectural marvel is integrated into its natural setting. Its lines forcibly follow those of the land, making it wind and double back like a great snake. Different materials were used according to the period: rammed earth was employed by the Western Han in Gansu province, whereas masonry (often brick) was favored by the Ming rulers of China. The Great Wall can be seen primarily as a form of military defense, but it also served to protect Chinese culture from outside influences. Despite the excessive development of tourist facilities near Badaling, the Great Wall on the whole has been well maintained, especially considering its length and complexity. This is surely not to say that long stretches have not disappeared, victim to erosion, the use of its stones for other construction, or the more destructive spread of "modern" buildings and roads.

Construction of defensive walls dates back even further in Chinese history than the Great Wall, as seen during the Chunqiu (722–481 B.C.) and Warring States (453–221 B.C.) periods. Vestiges of walls built by the Wei in 408 B.C. remain visible. The actual realization of the Great Wall began when parts of the walls built by the Qin, Zhao, and Yan kingdoms in the third century B.C. to defend against northern barbarians were restored and linked together by Qin Shi Huang (259–210 B.C.), the so-called First Emperor. Little remains of the construction from this period. By the time of the reign of Emperor Wudi (140–87

B.C.), the Great Wall already stretched for a length of about 3,728 miles (6,000 kilometers), from the Bohai Sea to Dunhuang. Work on the wall was substantially reduced after the end of the Han dynasty (220 A.D.), only to be revived by the Ming dynasty (1368–1644), which built a further 3,511 miles (5,650 kilometers) of its length, together with even more landscaped defensive works. Fortresses were added, and broad passages allowing the movement of soldiers became part of the design. Monuments were erected by the Ming to mark either end of the structure. The Great Wall was breached only in 1644, by the invading Manchus. As late as 2009, a length of 180 miles (290 kilometers) of the wall that had been built during the Ming period and covered by sand or the natural setting were rediscovered. The first known Western accounts of the Great Wall probably date from about 1605.

By modern standards, the Great Wall surely cost an exorbitant number of human lives in its construction, a form of accounting that has only recently been taken into account. A testimony to the history and culture of one of the greatest nations, the Great Wall is the clearest proof that architecture and civilization are intimately and permanently linked.

1546

Piazza del Campidoglio

ROME, ITALY

THE PIAZZA DEL CAMPIDOGLIO is located on the
Capitoline Hill, one of the seven famous hills of Rome.
Inhabited and built on from the earliest times of Rome,
the location of a number of temples, one of which was dedicated
to Jupiter, the hill was largely built over with palaces by the sixteenth century and is now the site of the Capitoline Museums.
Traditionally, the orientation of the buildings on the hill was in the
direction of the nearby Forum, representing the seat of Roman
power. The importance of the Capitoline Hill was again underlined in the Middle Ages, when it was the seat of city government.

Aside from its dense tissue of urban and architectural history,
the hill is the location of one of Michelangelo Buonarroti's most
significant architectural achievements, the Piazza del
Campidoglio. Planned for a visit by the Holy Roman Emperor
Charles V that was scheduled for 1538, the work on the square
was commissioned by Pope Paul III in 1536. Although the original
alignments in the direction of the Forum had been progressively
attenuated, Michelangelo's intervention affirmed a new orientation, with the piazza and the palaces surrounding it facing in the
direction of St. Peter's and parts of the city that were less filled
with reminiscences of ancient Rome. Around the sloped, trapezoidal square, a new oval pavement with a diamond design was
nonetheless created to receive a monumental equestrian statue
of Marcus Aurelius. The reason for this apparent contradiction is
that the statue had been thought to represent the first Christian
emperor. Michelangelo created the relatively modest base on
which the sculpture, now replaced with a replica, stood.

After Michelangelo's death, work on the square continued, in
particular for the palazzi, initially under the guidance of Tommaso
Cavalieri. The paving, created according to Michelangelo's documented design, was completed only in 1940, under the orders of
Benito Mussolini. Existing buildings—the Palazzo del Senatore
(built in the 13th and 14th centuries above the former Tabularium,
which had housed the archives of ancient Rome) and the Palazzo
dei Conservatori (built on top of the ruins of the Temple of Jupiter
in the Middle Ages)—were restored, and a new building, called
the Palazzo Nuovo (begun in 1603 and completed in 1654 according to Michelangelo's plans for the Palazzo dei Conservatori
facade) was added. The Palazzo Nuovo was meant as a mirror

image of the Palazzo dei Conservatori, whose facade Michelangelo
redesigned, giving formal balance to the entire composition. The
square can be approached from below via an axial stairway called
the Cordonata.

Because it was the site of the Temple of Jupiter at a time
when Rome really was the "center of the world," reference has
been made to the Campidoglio as being the *caput mundi*, or
"head of the world." The oval or, more precisely, egglike form
of Michelangelo's design for the paving of the square, placing
an emperor then thought to be the first Christian leader of
Rome in a direction facing St. Peter's Basilica, is redolent with
symbolism. Axial symmetry is sought, and it is clearly suggested
that the new world, that of Christendom, in a sense starts here.
Michelangelo the architect has made virtues of the "faults" of a
square that is irregular both in section and in plan, sloping, or
rather arcing, its horse-borne emperor finally a decorative element in an ingenious urban design.

MICHELANGELO RESURFACED THE
PALAZZO DEL SENATORE WITH TWO-
STORY GIANT ORDER CORINTHIAN
PILASTERS ABOVE A GROUND STORY
OF RUSTICATED STONE. HE ALSO
MOVED THE BELL TOWER TO ALIGN
AXIALLY WITH THE ENTRANCE,
CREATING A BOLD FOCUS FOR THE
COMPOSITION.

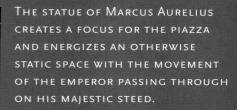

THE STATUE OF MARCUS AURELIUS
CREATES A FOCUS FOR THE PIAZZA
AND ENERGIZES AN OTHERWISE
STATIC SPACE WITH THE MOVEMENT
OF THE EMPEROR PASSING THROUGH
ON HIS MAJESTIC STEED.

MICHELANGELO MASTERFULLY
CORRECTED THE PERCEPTION OF
THE IRREGULAR TRAPEZOIDAL SPACE
INTO AN IDEALIZED GEOMETRY.
WHEN APPROACHED ON AXIS,
THE OVAL PAVING PATTERNS ARE
PERCEIVED AS A CIRCLE, AND THE
TWIN BUILDINGS SEEM TO FACE
EACH OTHER STRAIGHT ON, BUT IN
FACT ARE ANGLED TOWARDS EACH
OTHER.

1626

St. Peter's Basilica

ROME, ITALY

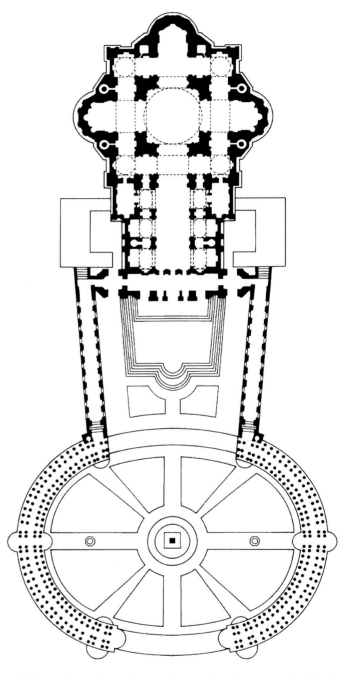

REACHING TO A HEIGHT of 453 feet (138 meters), the dome of St. Peter's, inspired by the Pantheon, spans 138 feet (42 meters). Located on the Tiber River, the church is still a majestic presence on the skyline of Rome, dominating the Vatican. It is not surprising that, given its size and significance, the structure required contributions by numerous architects, including Donato Bramante, Michelangelo, and Gian Lorenzo Bernini. It is thought to be the place of burial of St. Peter, the first bishop of Rome, and has been the site of Christian churches since the fourth century. The existing basilica was built beginning in 1506 on the foundations of Old St. Peter's Basilica, the fourth-century church created by Emperor Constantine. It was only in 1950 that Pope Pius XII announced that archeological work had identified the grave of the saint.

The age of the preceding basilica encouraged popes beginning with Nicholas V (reigned 1447–55) to envisage substantial work or reconstruction. Leon Battista Alberti and Bernardo Rossellino were called on at that time. It was Pope Julius II who decided in 1505 to demolish the older structure, in part to make way for his own mausoleum. A design based on a Greek cross with a great dome by Bramante was chosen by the pope the following year. With the death of Julius in 1513, plans for construction passed on to the great artist Raphael and the architect Giuliano da Sangallo and, subsequently, to Antonio da Sangallo. It was only in 1547 that Pope Paul III gave Michelangelo his supervisory role in the design.

Michelangelo's own scheme made use of the designs that had preceded his but gave the whole a new-found coherence. He redesigned the dome, apparently preferring an ovoid section as opposed to a more hemispheric one. The construction of the dome was completed in 1590. One of the last architects to influence the final design, in particular of the facade, was Carlo Maderno, who became involved in 1602. He was succeeded in 1629 by none other than Bernini, who is responsible for the elliptical "arms" that reach out to greet the faithful in St. Peter's Square in front of the basilica. Work on the new basilica lasted 120 years and cost so much that the sale of "indulgences" contributed to increasing religious opposition to the Roman Catholic church and to the rise of Martin Luther.

With such works as the nearly 100 foot (30 meter) tall baldachin of the altar of the pope designed by Bernini directly above the tomb of St. Peter, Michelangelo's *Pietà*, or indeed the great man's own contribution to the architecture, the basilica is home to some of the most celebrated works of art in the world. Place of burial of the popes, St. Peter's Basilica is certainly one of the most hallowed places in the Christian world. As is so often the case, its site is replete with historical references and precedents. In this case, even the building is the fruit of the collaboration over more than a century of some of the greatest architects and artists in Western history.

St. Peter's Basilica
Rome, Italy, 1626

(ABOVE)
Aerial view of the Basilica
of St. Peter's.

(RIGHT)
The dome of St. Peter's
designed by Michelangelo.

CA. 1440

Red Square

MOSCOW, RUSSIA

R ED SQUARE, surely one of the most famous public spaces in the world, is located east of the Kremlin and north of the banks of the Moskva River, with St. Basil's Cathedral (1554–60), built on orders of Ivan the Terrible (1530–1584), at its head. The major streets of Russia's capital find their point of origin in the square, highlighting its symbolic significance, which has been confirmed by the many official ceremonies held there, including those during the Soviet years. Its colorful name, Krasnaya Ploshchad in Russian, dates from 1661 and is apparently related to the double meaning of the word krasnaya, which can translate as either "red" or "beautiful." Prior to the seventeenth century, the square was called the Torg, or Market, before being named Trinity Square for Trinity Cathedral, which stood on the site of St. Basil's before the latter's construction.

Red Square's physical origin is related to the history of the Kremlin and orders given in the late fifteenth century by Ivan the Great (1440–1505) to clear all construction from an area (234 square meters; 768 feet) in front of newly built walls. A white stone platform (known as *Lobnoye mesto*) erected in the sixteenth century was the place from which edicts and decrees were read, and it was from here that the tsar presented himself to the people once a year. Long a central market space for the city, the square retains this element of its history with the rather unexpected presence of the famous state department store, GUM (built 1888–93; privatized in 1993), situated on the eastern side of the square, opposite the Kremlin walls. The last remaining wooden structures were removed in 1679 and 1680, and the square was paved in stone in 1804; in 1892 it was illuminated by lanterns for the first time.

Used for military parades by the Soviets beginning in 1919, Red Square has been the location of the tomb of Lenin since the stone mausoleum, designed by Alexei Shchusev, was completed in 1930. During that same year, the square's cobblestone paving was replaced with granite. Events held on Red Square, such as

the 1945 Victory Parade when Nazi flags were piled beneath the tomb of Lenin, have marked recent history, as have the staid but rather frightening annual October displays of military hardware that were a "highlight" of the cold war. Over time, numerous buildings have come and gone along the periphery of the square, such as Kazan Cathedral (built in 1620, demolished in the 1930s, and rebuilt in 1993). Plans were laid at the time of Stalin to demolish St. Basil's Cathedral, a monument preserved only at the personal request of the leader. The northern edge of the square has been occupied by the State Historical Museum since its establishment in 1872.

Red Square, which is 1,083 feet (330 meters) long and 230 feet (70 meters) wide, was inscribed on the UNESCO World Heritage List in 1990, together with the Kremlin, because of its historical significance. Since the fall of the Soviet Union, the square has assumed other functions aside from the normal flow of tourism—rock concerts and other large-scale events such as fashion shows are performed there on a regular basis.

CA. 1670

Palace of Versailles

VERSAILLES, FRANCE

THE CHÂTEAU DE VERSAILLES, one of the most extravagant architectural endeavors of the French monarchy, started life as a relatively modest hunting lodge located 12.5 miles (20 kilometers) southwest of Paris. The pavilion was built for King Louis XIII (reigned 1610–43) beginning in 1623. It was his successor Louis XIV (reigned 1643–1715) who undertook a massive expansion of the site in order to officially establish the court there in 1682. The reasons for this move were surely multiple. The palace not only became a showplace for the authority and culture of the French monarchy, and of the "Sun King" in particular, but it also served a political purpose, obliging the sometimes-rebellious nobles to be grouped around the king rather than plotting against him elsewhere. The Château de Versailles as it exists today has a floor area of 721,180 square feet (67,000 square meters) and no fewer than 2,300 rooms.

It is not surprising that some of the most talented architects and artists of the time participated in the design, construction, and decoration of Versailles. A first group of these emerged from the fall of Nicolas Fouquet (1615–1680), who, as superintendent of finances from 1653 to 1661, built the splendid Château de Vaux-le-Vicomte, deemed far too extravagant by the king, who terminated Fouquet's mandate in 1661. The architect Louis Le Vau (1612–1670), the painter Charles Le Brun (1619–1690), and, perhaps most significantly, the landscape architect André Le Nôtre (1613–1700) all worked on Vaux-le-Vicomte and were enlisted by the king for his new palace in Versailles.

Between 1669 and 1672, the *grands appartements*— the state rooms of the king and queen—and other new areas were built by Le Vau and decorated by Le Brun and others, including furniture designers such as André-Charles Boulle (1642–1732), author amongst other works of the mirrored walls, wood mosaic floors, and marquetry furniture of the Cabinet du Dauphin (1682–86). Le Nôtre, the prototypical landscape architect, was responsible for much of the grand, axial garden design still visible at Versailles. Although historians emphasize the influence of Italian culture on developments in seventeenth-century France, Versailles was almost completely new in its grandeur and emphasis on a complete design.

Construction continued with such noted architects as Jules Hardouin-Mansart, who designed the Orangerie and the north and south wings of the palace as well as the celebrated Hall of Mirrors (Galerie des Glaces), which measures nearly 240 feet (73 meters) long. At the beginning of the new century, a royal chapel designed by Hardouin-Mansart was completed by Robert de Cotte in 1710. The subsequent kings, Louis XV (Opera, Petit Trianon) and Louis XVI, also contributed to the royal residence and seat of power, but not to the extent of Louis XIV. Great sales of the furniture of Versailles were held after the French Revolution between 1793 and 1795, rendering it much more difficult to really perceive the glory that was Versailles. In the early nineteenth century Versailles underwent new changes, becoming the museum of the history of France, dedicated to "all the glories" of the country, as ordered in 1830 by Louis-Philippe, then king of France.

More than a work of architecture, the Palace of Versailles is an early example of what the Germans have called *Gesamtkunstwerk*—the total work of art. Architecture, of course, but also the works of fine art, furniture design, landscape architecture, and even the ephemeral arts associated with grand parties and theatrical events, all were part of the spirit and creation that was Versailles. It is no accident that Versailles remains among the most visited tourist sites of France.

1620–63

Katsura Imperial Villa

KYOTO, JAPAN

PRINCE TOSHIHITO, the creator of Katsura, was born in 1579. The younger brother of Emperor Goyozei, Toshihito showed interest from an early age in literature, particularly *The Tale of Genji*. Written just after 1000 A.D., *The Tale of Genji*, which chronicles the life of an ideal courtier, is considered by some to be the first novel. Little is known about its author, Murasaki Shikibu, except that she was the daughter of a provincial governor and lived roughly between 973 and 1025.

Murasaki could hardly have imagined that six centuries later her words would be at the origin of one of Japan's great works of art and architecture, the Imperial Villa of Katsura. In the chapter of her work entitled "The Wind in the Pines" Murasaki wrote: "Far away, in the country village of Katsura, the reflection of the moon upon the water is clear and tranquil." As circumstances would have it, land south of the Katsura River near Kyoto came into the hands of Toshihito, who surely was aware of its literary significance. The area had also been the site of a residence modeled on the villa of the Tang-era poet Bai Juyi (772–846). Bai Juyi's poem "The Song of Everlasting Regret" (806) figures prominently in *The Tale of Genji*. Little more than a melon patch when Toshihito began to transform the area, it was described in the records of Shokoku-ji Temple in 1631 as a "palace" used for moon-viewing parties based on *The Tale of Genji*.

Toshihito died in 1629, and by 1642 his son Prince Toshitada began to renovate and expand the original structures. Toshitada expressed his desire to make Katsura into an ideal place for the tea ceremony, and he built several additional teahouses on the grounds. He also explicitly mentioned his wish to make the garden similar to the one in *The Tale of Genji*. Although some sources give credit to the tea ceremony master and architect Kobori Enshu for the design of Katsura, it was also the product of the active interests of the princes who developed it progressively. As early as the fourteenth century, the cultivated nobility of Japan had rejected ornate architecture in favor of a

search for harmony with nature, and Katsura represents an apogee of this aesthetic sensibility called the *sukiya* style.

Toshitada died in 1662, and his successors did not live long enough to continue work on the Imperial Villa. When the family line died out in 1883, Katsura became a domain of the emperor, but for historic reasons it fell into disrepair. Like many historic buildings in other countries, Katsura was not fully appreciated by the Japanese until the architect Bruno Taut arrived in Japan in 1933 at the invitation of the Japanese Association for International Architecture. Such was its state of neglect that on November 4, 1935, Taut wrote, "I can claim to be the 'discoverer' of Katsura."

Taut and then Le Corbusier and Gropius were fascinated by Katsura's "modernity." They saw its undecorated orthogonal and modular spaces as parallels to contemporary modernism, going so far as to identify Katsura as a "historical" example of modernity. The modernists saw what they wanted to see in Katsura—the Mondrian-like simplicity of certain designs—while looking less at its rustic side, or at the "complexity and contradiction" that lie in almost every aspect of the buildings and gardens.

Katsura Imperial Villa
Kyoto, Japan, 1620–63

(RIGHT)
The interior of the Katsura Imperial Villa exemplifies the geometric order characteristic of Zen Buddhist aesthetics.

1635

Queen's House

GREENWICH, ENGLAND

INIGO JONES (1573–1652) is considered one of the great architects of England. He was responsible for the design of Covent Garden square as well as the Palladian-style Whitehall Banqueting House (1622). The architect was also a designer of court spectacles and became Surveyor of the King's Works in 1613.

In 1616 Jones was asked to design a private pavilion in Greenwich for Anne of Denmark, queen consort of King James I. Influenced by time he had spent in Italy in 1613–15, Jones created a design apparently modeled on that of the Medici villa in Poggio a Caiano (built beginning in 1485 by Giuliano de Sangallo, 1443–1516). The death of Anne of Denmark in 1619 halted work on the house in Greenwich near the red brick Tudor Palace of Greenwich. The structure was altered and completed in 1635 by Jones when the property came under the control of Henrietta Maria of France, wife of Charles I and daughter of Henry IV. Works of art purchased by Charles I from the Gonzaga family in Mantua were used to decorate the house, while artists such as Orazio Gentileschi (1563–1639) and Jacob Jordaens (1593–1678) were granted commissions for ceiling paintings. Though much of the decor was displaced after the execution of the king in 1649, the basic proportions and mathematical design of the Queen's House, clearly inspired by the Palladian or classical example, represent a significant development in architecture in England of the time. Henrietta Maria returned to the house in 1662, shortly after her son Charles II took the throne. The new king had upper-level rooms that bridged over a road added to the original design.

In an interesting continuation of the artistic history of this residence, Willem van de Velde the Elder (ca. 1611–1693) and his son Willem van de Velde the Younger (1633–1707) established their studio in the Queen's House when they began to work on marine paintings for Charles II. Their presence in London up

until 1692 was the basis for the creation of the English school of marine painting in the eighteenth and nineteenth centuries. Beginning in 1674, the two artists were given a south-facing room for their studio and used the upper floor of the house to lay out tapestry designs.

King George III granted the Queen's House to the Royal Naval Asylum in 1805. The architect Daniel Asher made additions for dormitories and classrooms in the period 1807–12, and it was finally taken over by the National Maritime Museum in 1934. Restored from 1933 to 1937 in order to display the early collections of the museum, the residence was again renovated in the 1990s. It has been used since 2001 for the museum's fine art collection, although it has served other functions such as being the VIP center for the 2012 Olympic Games. The Queen's House is a Grade I listed building and a Scheduled Ancient Monument. The entire group of buildings at Greenwich and the park in which they are set, originally designed by André Le Nôtre, include the former Royal Naval College by Christopher Wren and the Old Royal Observatory by Wren and the scientist Robert Hooke.

THE QUEEN'S HOUSE FACES THE
RIVER THAMES AND LOOKS
TOWARD LONDON. WHEN SIR
CHRISTOPHER WREN PLANNED
THE SITE FOR GREENWICH
HOSPITAL (LATER THE OLD ROYAL
NAVAL COLLEGE), THE VIEW OF
THE RIVER WAS FRAMED BY TWO
BAROQUE TOWERS.

THE COLONNADE MARKS THE
LOCATION OF THE MAIN ROAD
FROM LONDON TO DOVER, WHICH
ORIGINALLY RAN BETWEEN THE
TWO WINGS. AS BUILT BY JONES,
THE HOUSE WAS IN THE SHAPE OF
AN H, WITH ITS TWO SECTIONS
CONNECTED BY A BRIDGE ON THE
UPPER STORY. AFTER JONES'S
DEATH, HIS STUDENT JOHN WEBB
ADDED TWO BRIDGES TO MAKE
THE BUILDING CUBE SHAPED.

JONES WAS INSPIRED BY THE
WRITINGS AND BUILDINGS OF
ANDREA PALLADIO IN DESIGNING
THE FIRST TRUE RENAISSANCE
BUILDING IN ENGLAND. THE
NORTH AND SOUTH FACADES ARE
TRIPARTITE, WITH THE CENTER
SECTION PROJECTING SLIGHTLY
FROM THE SIDES. THE BUILDING'S
BEAUTY LIES IN ITS EXQUISITE
PROPORTIONS AND FORMAL
SYMMETRY.

1648

Taj Mahal

AGRA, UTTAR PRADESH, INDIA

THE TAJ MAHAL was the last and greatest architectural and artistic achievement of the Mughal period in Agra, before its builder, Shah Jehan (1592–1658), shifted his capital to what is now Delhi. History has concentrated on the idea that the Taj Mahal is a monument to love because it was erected beginning in 1632 in honor of Shah Jehan's third wife, Arjumand Banu Begum, yet the monument and its gardens carry a clear evocation of paradise as defined in the Quran and Islamic symbolism. Indeed, verses from the Quran inlaid in stone adorn both the gates and the Taj Mahal itself.

According to Islam there are four rivers in paradise, a concept at the origin of the Persian *charbagh* style of garden planning. Having passed through the main gate, itself an evocation of the entrance to paradise, the visitor to the Taj Mahal discovers two marble canals that cross in the center of the garden, dividing it into four equal squares. The Taj Mahal itself is elevated on a 313.3 foot (95.5 meter) square plinth at the distant end of the garden. The majestic dome that dominates the structure is placed in the center of this square and forms a perfect circle. It has frequently been written that in the symbolism of Islam, a square represents man, and a circle the divine. Leonardo da Vinci's *Vitruvian Man* is of course inscribed in a circle and a square, giving a humanist interpretation to shapes used by the Mughals to other ends; yet, despite being years and continents apart, art and architecture fuse around the same essential forms. The fact that different religions and civilizations produce such similarities of symbolism and form is more than coincidence; it is proof of how deeply rooted are the ties between various other forms of artistic expression and architecture. The plan of the actual tomb chamber of Mumtaz Mahal and Shah Jahan is a perfect octagon, with the cenotaph of Mumtaz Mahal placed at the center. Installed more than thirty years later, the cenotaph of Shah Jehan is placed to the west of that of his wife.

Located on the Yamuna River in a 42 acre (17 hectare) garden, the Taj Mahal is considered one of the most beautiful realizations of Indo-Islamic architecture. The structure is perfectly symmetrical along the central axis. Brick-in lime-mortar is veneered with red sandstone and white Makrana marble from Jodhpur, with inlays of semiprecious and precious stones. In 1983, the Taj Mahal became a UNESCO World Heritage Site. The international organization's description of the building reads, in part, the "Taj Mahal represents the finest architectural and artistic achievement through perfect harmony and excellent craftsmanship in a whole range of Indo-Islamic sepulchral architecture. It is a masterpiece of architectural style in conception, treatment and execution and has unique aesthetic qualities in balance, symmetry and harmonious blending of various elements."

Aside from the garden and the tomb itself, the complex includes a number of other structures. One of these is the *darwaza*, or main gateway, a three-story red sandstone structure completed in 1648. On the east and west sides of the tomb are two identical red sandstone buildings. One of these is a mosque that sanctifies the area and provides a place of worship. The other, called the *jawab*, may have been used as a guesthouse but also preserves the architectural balance of the composition.

1674

Les Invalides

PARIS, FRANCE

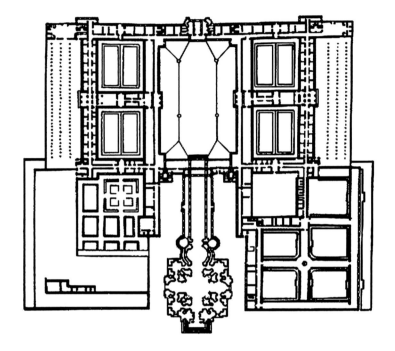

THE HÔTEL NATIONAL des Invalides is located on the axis of the Alexander III bridge on the Left Bank of the Seine in Paris. The wide green space that stretches from the building all the way to the bridge is called the Esplanade des Invalides, designed by the architect Robert de Cotte (1656–1735) in 1704. Since the nineteenth century, the structure has contained the Musée de l'Armée (Museum of the French Army) as well as the tomb of Emperor Napoleon I. The Institution Nationale des Invalides for war veterans is still housed in the complex.

It was in 1670, on the instructions of King Louis XIV, that plans were made to create a hospital for war veterans on a nearly 25 acre (10 hectare) site in the middle of Paris. The main structure was designed by Libéral Bruant (1635–1697) with a facade facing the Seine no less than 643 feet (196 meters) in length. Work began in 1670 and was completed four years later, though the church was built only beginning in 1676. Bruant was also the architect of the Pitié-Salpêtrière (1660) in Paris that is now a hospital, as well as of the Place Vendôme. The Cathedral of Saint-Louis des Invalides, in the form of a Greek cross, was designed within the complex by a student of Bruant, Jules Hardouin-Mansart (1646–1708), and was inaugurated by Louis XIV on August 28, 1706. The double-shelled dome with an oculus at the summit was inspired by St. Peter's in Rome. The centrally placed dome reaches a height of 351 feet (107 meters) and looks down on the *cour d'honneur*, the largest of the fifteen courtyards in the complex, where significant military funerals are held. The plan of the Invalides is believed to be related to that of the Escorial (1584) near Madrid. The interior decor of the dome was painted by Charles de La Fosse (1636–1715), a pupil of Charles Le Brun. The dome of the Invalides was covered in gold leaf for the first time in 1715. Napoleon had it regilded in 1807, and it was restored and again covered with gold in 1937. The most recent restoration work, accompanied by the application of 27.8 pounds (12.6 kilograms) of gold leaf, dates from 1989.

Exiled on the island of Saint Helena beginning in 1815, Napoleon I died in 1821. His remains were kept there until 1840,

when King Louis-Philippe ordered them returned to Paris. A national funeral was organized, and the corpse was brought to the Invalides. The king asked the architect Louis Visconti (1791–1853), who would later work on the Louvre, to design a tomb for the emperor, in which his remains were placed in 1861. The openly visible red quartzite sarcophagus is lifted up on a green granite base and located directly under the great dome of Hardouin-Mansart. A number of other military celebrities of France are buried in the Invalides, including the noted military engineer Sébastien Le Prestre de Vauban (1633–1707), whose ashes were placed there at the request of Napoleon I in 1808.

Aside from influencing the creation of Greenwich Hospital, founded in 1694 as the Royal Hospital for Seamen at Greenwich and designed by Christopher Wren, the Invalides, and in particular its dome, apparently had an impact on the design of the dome of the U.S. Capitol in Washington, D.C. (designed by Thomas Walter; 1866), the U.S. Naval Academy Chapel in Annapolis, Maryland (1908), and San Francisco City Hall (1915), as well as numerous other structures across the world.

Les Invalides
Paris, France, 1674

(RIGHT)
Église du Dôme rising behind the main courtyard of Hôtel National des Invalides.

1697

St. Paul's Cathedral

LONDON, ENGLAND

LIKE OTHER SIGNIFICANT CHURCHES in Europe, St. Paul's Cathedral was built on the site of several previous structures on Ludgate Hill. The first known church in London dedicated to St. Paul was a wooden structure built in 604 a.d. by King Ethelbert of Kent. A stone church succeeded it on the same spot at the end of that same century. Destroyed by fire twice, in 962 and 1087, it was rebuilt and then extended and renovated in the thirteenth and fourteenth centuries, confirming its place as one of the largest cathedrals in Europe. Inigo Jones added the west front of the cathedral in the 1630s. Christopher Wren made a design for the renovation of the Gothic structure in 1665, only to see the old building destroyed in the Great Fire of London in 1666. Wren was named Surveyor of Works in 1669 and given the task of rebuilding a total of fifty-two churches, though Nicholas Hawksmoor designed some of these. Built between 1675 and 1711, St. Paul's Cathedral was something of a hybrid of designs proposed by the architect to the Bishop of London. These ranged from a Greek cross plan with an enormous central dome to the Latin cross plan finally adapted with a somewhat smaller dome. In 1673 he produced the so-called Great Model, an oak and plaster 20 foot (6 meter) long reproduction of the cathedral design, which was presented to King Charles II.

The 364 foot (111 meter) high triple dome that was finally built was the highest structure in London until 1962, and it is supported by eight arches. The style of the Portland stone building is described as English baroque but bears comparison to Saint Peter's Basilica in Rome. Wren certainly studied the architecture of France and the drawings of Bernini in 1665.

Aside from its long dominance of the London skyline, St. Paul's Cathedral has also influenced urban development through the action of the London View Management Framework that stipulates that certain sight lines allowing views of the famous dome must be kept unencumbered by other buildings. Wren's own words, "Architecture aims at eternity," might best be applied to his own creation.

Aside from his role as Surveyor of Works, Wren was also an astronomer and mathematician. He acted as a professor of astronomy at Oxford from 1661 to 1673, precisely at the moment he was working on designs for Saint Paul's. In 1660 he was a founding member of the Royal Society. His other architectural work includes the Greenwich Royal Observatory (1676), Greenwich Hospital (1696–1715), work on Hampton Court Palace (1689–1702) and Kensington Palace.

Struck by German bombs on October 10, 1940, and April 17, 1941, the cathedral survived World War II less damaged than might have been the case if other explosive devices that reached it had detonated properly. A broad spectrum of the great and famous of England, such as Lord Nelson and the Duke of Wellington, is buried within its walls. Christopher Wren (1632–1723) also rests within what he called his "greatest work." The cathedral continues to be the location of events that are important for the nation, such as the funeral of Winston Churchill in 1965 and the marriage in 1981 of Prince Charles and Lady Diana Spencer.

1784

Monticello

Near Charlottesville, Virginia

Born in 1743 in Shadwell, Virginia, Thomas Jefferson is best known as the author of the Declaration of Independence and the third president of the United States. He began to build his home, Monticello, in 1769 on a hill in the midst of the 5,000 acre (2,023 hectare) plantation that he inherited.

Though not trained as an architect, he completed a first design for the house with a floor area of about 11,000 square feet (1,021 square meters) in 1784, before leaving Virginia to become minister (ambassador) of the United States in Paris. The brick and limestone mortar structure was enlarged between 1796 and 1809, possibly as a result of the architecture that Jefferson saw in Europe. The octagonal dome above a small room (the Dome Room) was added during this second building campaign, which occurred during his tenure as president of the United States (1801–9). As president, Jefferson showed himself favorable to architecture inspired by the classical world, in the mode of the Greek revival style practiced by Benjamin Henry Latrobe, whom he appointed as surveyor of public buildings in 1803.

Monticello is a U.S. National Historic Landmark and was also inscribed in 1987, together with the University of Virginia, on the UNESCO World Heritage List. Late in his life, Jefferson founded the University of Virginia and designed its buildings, again according to ideals of architecture that surely have their origin in European neoclassicism. The neoclassical design of Monticello is based on the ideas of Andrea Palladio. The UNESCO description of Monticello reads, in part, "The very personal conception of the house clearly shows the various influences experienced by its designer: that of Palladio, evidencing in the perfect proportions of the pedimented porticos, and that of the contemporary neoclassical architecture. The interior spatial organization and the low elevation were borrowed from contemporary Parisian town house design. The western side is dominated by an octagonal dome. Only the harmonious volume of the villa emerges from the foliage of the park where, towards the end of his life, Jefferson planted orchards and vegetable gardens." A cloth at the entrance to the house was painted green on the suggestion of the painter Gilbert Stuart so that the proximity

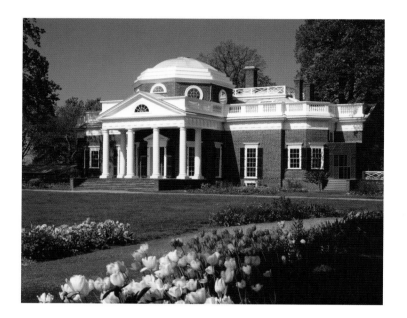

of nature to the house would be emphasized. Both the placement of the residence and its design give the visitor the impression of being at the center of the natural setting. The hilltop location and natural setting of Monticello, as well as its architecture, are said to be influenced by Palladio's Villa Rotonda (Villa Almerico Capra, Vicenza, Italy; 1571), and its basically cruciform plan is similar to that of London's Chiswick House (1729). The natural setting and the use of brick do make Monticello somewhat gentler in appearance than its English "cousin." Jefferson was buried on the grounds of Monticello. Today, the Thomas Jefferson Foundation operates Monticello and its grounds as a house museum and educational institution.

Though many political leaders and heads of state have been fascinated by architecture, few if any practiced it in the way that Jefferson did at Monticello and the University of Virginia. His use of the Palladian example is an expression of the nobility with which he wanted to invest the United States in its formative years. Monticello's architecture is an expression of clarity in design and of the ideal of man as the center of the world, concepts that emerged from the thoughts of the Renaissance, as seen in Leonardo da Vinci's drawing *Vitruvian Man* and, later, in Palladio's work.

1830

Altes Museum

BERLIN, GERMANY

THE ALTES MUSEUM in Berlin was built between 1823 and 1830 and designed by Karl Friedrich Schinkel (1781–1841). It is considered to be one of the most significant works of neoclassical architecture in Europe. Clearly influenced by Greek architecture with eighteen Ionic columns along its 285-foot (87 meter) long facade, the Altes Museum also bears the trace of Roman influence with the interior dome, originally a hemisphere inspired by the Pantheon. The dome is intentionally not visible from the exterior to avoid any competition with the nearby Berliner Dom.

An interesting aspect of the building is that its three other facades are designed with brick and stone bands without reference to the classical orders of architecture. The classical elements of the building, which is raised on a plinth, together with a monumental staircase, may evoke a palatial vocabulary more than one for a museum, but this is in relation to ideas of the time that Schinkel fully supported, but also surely to the proximity of the royal palace. It is, in a sense, a temple dedicated to art. The influence of this idea, and indeed of the relation of the display of art to education, makes the Altes Museum a pioneering institution that emerged at a time when the "modern" museum did not yet really exist.

Aside from being a celebrated architect, Schinkel was also a painter and city planner who created stage designs and furniture. His most famous works include the Neue Wache (New Guard House; 1816–18); the National Monument for the Liberation Wars (1818–21); the Schauspielhaus (Theater; 1819–21) at the Gendarmenmarkt; and the Altes Museum, located on the Museumsinsel, which eventually became the home of five museums. The plan for the island, drawn up in 1841 by the architect Friedrich August Stüler, led to the creation of the Neues Museum (1843–47); the Nationalgalerie, by Johann Heinrich Strack (1866); the Kaiser-Friedrich-Museum by Ernst von Ihne

(now the Bodemuseum; 1897–1904), and finally the Pergamonmuseum by Alfred Messel (1909–30).

It is emphasized in the history of Schinkel's work that his knowledge of architectural types was of great importance in his designs, but so, too, was his friendship with a certain number of leading intellectual figures of his time. One of these was Wilhelm von Humboldt (1767–1835), the philosopher and founder of the University of Berlin. Schinkel first met Humboldt in 1803 in Italy. Later head of the Commission for the Establishment of the Altes Museum, Humboldt and his brother Alexander made museums part of the goals of the Prussian educational system, which they are credited with establishing.

Originally created to house all of Berlin's art collections, the two-story Altes Museum has been reserved for the display of classical antiquities since 1904. Seriously damaged by fire during World War II, it was rebuilt in 1966. The rectangular building has galleries arrayed around two inner courts and the central domed rotunda. Until 1845, it was called the Königliches Museum (Royal Museum). Along with the other museums and historic buildings on Museum Island, the Altes Museum was listed as a UNESCO World Heritage Site in 1999.

Altes Museum
Berlin, Germany, 1830

(ABOVE)
The oculus at the top of the coffered dome provides natural light for the central rotunda of the museum. Although roughly one-half the size, Schinkel's design was inspired by the Pantheon in Rome.

(RIGHT)
"Löwenkämpfer" ("Lion-fighter") completed by Albert Wolff in 1861 after an initial design by Christian Daniel Rauch. One of two statues that flank the entrance staircase to the museum.

(FAR RIGHT)
Aerial view of Altes Museum, Berlin, Germany, 1830

1883

Sagrada Familia Basilica

BARCELONA, SPAIN

THE SAGRADA FAMILIA church might be called one of the strangest monuments of the Catholic faith. It is certainly a unique work in the history of ecclesiastic architecture. It was designed by the Catalan architect Antoni Gaudí (1852–1926), whose artistic style and originality are undisputed, but it will not be finished until long after his lifetime. In fact, only a quarter of the basilica had been completed at the time of his death. It is true that the architect reconciled himself to this fact, saying famously, "Don't worry, my client is not in a hurry." His organic and even whimsical forms seem closer to surrealism than they do to art nouveau, for example, even though they have roots in Gothic architecture. Even the pace of construction, once reckoned to require centuries, is in keeping with the ways in which Gothic cathedrals took form. Work began on the church in 1882, and despite not being completed, the basilica was consecrated by Pope Benedict XVI on November 7, 2010.

Works such as his Parque Güell in Barcelona (1900–14) employ a profusion of colorful broken tiles that sometimes resolve themselves into explicitly biomorphic designs like the python dragon that guards the park. Dalí found in it many of the roots of surrealism and emphasized the profound religious content of Gaudí's work. Gaudí himself, who became religious only in his forties, said, "Those who look for the laws of nature as a support for their new works collaborate with the creator."

Gaudí, having studied Gothic architecture, set out to correct its "faults." He called the external supports, such as flying buttresses, "crutches" and considered the structures to be overly complex and fragile. He also felt that the use of wood in roof design rendered Gothic churches too vulnerable to insects, humidity, and fire. He sought to eliminate exterior structural elements and to employ branched columns in the image of a tree. The interior columns branch out, but they also change form, evolving as they rise. In a way, Gaudí's design could be considered a harbinger of the kind of extremely complex forms that computer-assisted design allows for today. This is also true of the manufacturing techniques concerned. Whereas unique stone blocks for the church formerly had to be individually carved, today's CNC milling techniques make it seem feasible to complete the church as "early" as 2026.

The church plan is that of a Latin cross with five aisles. The central nave vaults reach 148 feet (45 meters). Gaudí originally imagined no less than eighteen spires for the church, but only eight had been built as of 2010. Although Gaudí's intentions for the form of the church are known, newer elements, such as figurative sculptures created by Josep Maria Subirachs and others after 1987 on one facade have been actively opposed. The principal face of the church, called the Glory Facade, began construction in 2002. Construction goes on in good part thanks to the entrance fees paid by approximately two million visitors a year, which is to say more than the Alhambra in Grenada or the Prado Museum in Madrid.

1889

Eiffel Tower

PARIS, FRANCE

INITIALLY DESIGNED to stand just twenty years, the Eiffel Tower remained the tallest building in the world from 1889 to 1930, when it was surpassed by New York's Chrysler Building. Together with its antenna array, the three-story structure, built in just two years, today reaches a total height of 1,063 feet (324 meters). The tower, built as the entrance arch to the 1889 Universal Exhibition, is named after the French engineer Gustave Eiffel, whose own Compagnie des établissements Eiffel built it. Eiffel also designed such monuments as the Maria Pia Bridge in Porto, Portugal (1877), at the time the longest single-arch span bridge in the world. Eiffel's original company still exists, several mergers later under the name Eiffage Construction Métallique. It has worked on such varied structures as the Channel Tunnel (1994), the Louvre Pyramid (1989), and the Millau Viaduct (2004). In an interesting twist, the viaduct is now actually the tallest structure in France, surpassing the Eiffel Tower.

Although it has been asserted that the forms of the Eiffel Tower were the result more of an empirical approach than of very precise calculations, the resistance of the structure over time and to wind loads demonstrates that the engineering was fundamentally sound and elegant in its somewhat unexpected solutions. Even the original elevators continued to function long beyond their intended use. They were replaced in 1982 after 97 years of service.

Gustave Eiffel initially showed little enthusiasm for a design that originated with other engineers in his firm, Maurice Koechlin and Émile Nouguier, and an architect named Stephen Sauvestre. The scheme was first shown in Paris at the Exhibition of Decorative Arts in 1884. During a formal presentation made to the Society of Engineers (Société des Ingiénieurs Civils) in 1885, Eiffel vaunted the structure as one that would glorify "not only the art of the modern engineer, but also the century of industry and science in which we are living, and for which the way was prepared by the great scientific movement of the eighteenth century." An 1886 competition duly chose Eiffel as the designer for the centerpiece of the Universal Exposition. The decision was met with a flurry of protests based on aesthetic, functional, or practical considerations, with the tower being labeled "useless and monstrous" by a worthy committee of three hundred architects and artists.

Concrete slabs were created to support the legs of the tower beginning in early 1887, and foundation work was completed by the end of June. Partially preassembled iron elements were manufactured in Levallois-Perret, and such innovations as a small crane that could move up the structure as it advanced, or careful safety procedures to protect workers, were employed. The four legs of the tallest structure in the world were joined in March 1888. A first group of officials was brought by Eiffel to the uppermost deck of the tower on foot on March 31, 1889. More than two million persons visited it in the course of the exhibition. With 7.1 million visitors in 2011, the Eiffel Tower remains the most-visited paying monument in the world. Aside from observation areas, the tower has always included restaurants or a bar with sweeping views of the city. The present tenants are 58 Tour Eiffel on the first level above the ground, and the Jules Verne Restaurant on the second level, 125 meters above the Champ de Mars.

1898

Secession Hall

VIENNA, AUSTRIA

THE VIENNA SECESSION (Vereinigung Bildender Künstler Österreichs) was founded in 1897 by a group of artists and architects, including Gustav Klimt (first chairman of the group), Josef Hoffmann, Joseph Maria Olbrich, and Koloman Moser, who broke with the conservative Association of Austrian Artists. Other figures such as Egon Schiele marked the movement as well. One of their first steps in 1897 was to appoint the young architect Olbrich (1867–1908) to design an exhibition hall (Wiener Secessionsgebäude) which would serve as part of their manifesto. Olbrich had been working for Otto Wagner since 1893, and his schemes met with a negative reaction from the town council, in part because of the very visible site chosen on the Ringstrasse. At the end of 1897, the city approved the building for another site on Friedrichstrasse, but only as a temporary exhibition pavilion with a ten-year lifespan.

The building, financed in part by the steel tycoon Karl Wittgenstein (father of the philosopher Ludwig Wittgenstein), was built in just six months between April and October 1898. Klimt made a sketch for the uppermost part of the building with its inscription "To every age its art, to art its freedom" (*Der Zeit ihre Kunst. Der Kunst ihre Freiheit*). A open work metal dome representing golden laurel leaves is suspended between four pylons. Three gorgons placed over the entrance symbolize architecture, sculpture, and painting. To emphasize and explain their thoughts, between 1898 and 1903, the group published an internal magazine called *Ver Sacrum* (Sacred Spring), with illustrations by Klimt, Moser, Hoffmann, and Alfred Roller, among others. Its literary contributors included Rainer Maria Rilke and Knut Hamsun. *Ver Sacrum* was a remarkable collaborative publication whose creation was influenced by the German magazine *Pan* (1895–1900), edited by Julius Meier-Graefe, with articles by figures such as Henry van de Velde and Nietzsche.

Among the exhibitions held in the building, the first one in November 1898 included works not only of Klimt, Moser or Olbrich, but also by Charles Rennie Mackintosh, Edgar Degas,

Giovanni Segantini, Edvard Munch, Vincent van Gogh, Paul Gauguin, or Auguste Rodin. As is often the case, the artists of a period who are making change happen know and recognize one another. In the case of the Secession, painting, sculpture, and design were at one with architecture.

One of the most famous, the fourteenth Secession exhibition (1902), was directed by Josef Hoffmann and included twenty-one artists in the intention of uniting the arts, where architecture, sculpture, and painting would come together. Gustav Klimt contributed his celebrated Beethoven Frieze to the building at that time. A sculpture by Max Klinger representing Beethoven occupied a place of honor, and no less than 60,000 persons came to view the show. The reason for the emphasis on Beethoven was that the members of the Secession believed that his work approached the concept of the *Gesamtkunstwerk*, the total work of art.

Applied arts were also of great importance to members of the Secession. Joseph Hoffmann and Koloman Moser founded the Wiener Werkstätte in 1903. Klimt, Hoffmann, Moser, and others left the Secession in 1905. This so-called Klimt Group held exhibitions in 1908 in the Kunstschau, a temporary pavilion designed by Josef Hoffmann.

Secession Hall
Vienna, Austria, 1898

(ABOVE)
Secession Hall, Vienna, Austria, 1898. Architect Josef Maria Olbrich

(RIGHT)
Entrance to the Secession Hall in Vienna, Austria, often described as the first architectural work of the Vienna Secession whose members included Otto Wagner, Josef Hoffman, Gustav Klimt, Josef Hoffman, and Josef Maria Olbrich.

DER · ZEIT · IHRE · KVNST ·
DER · KVNST · IHRE · FREIHEIT ·

MALEREI ARCHITEKTVR PLASTIK

1909

Glasgow School of Art

GLASGOW, SCOTLAND

CHARLES RENNIE MACKINTOSH was born in 1868 in Glasgow. After working with a local firm called Honeyman and Keppie, where he designed his first major architectural project, the Glasgow Herald building of 1899, he attempted without great success to create his own office in 1913. The Herald building, renamed "The Lighthouse," became Scotland's Center for Design and Architecture in 1999. Mackintosh adhered to ideas called "modernist" at the time, though not those later associated with the modernist movement in architecture. Rather, he pressed for design that was functional and made use of new technology, without constant reference to the past. He combined this conviction with participation in the arts and crafts movement in the United Kingdom and was thus logically a proponent of the floral style of art nouveau.

His international reputation was established by his design for the Glasgow School of Art (1897–1909). Honeyman and Keppie was selected for the job based on Mackintosh's 1896 competition entry. The architect's task was facilitated by the presence of Francis Newbury, director of the school, a former teacher and friend. Set on a rather difficult sloping site, the block-long structure was built with brick and masonry. Reference is apparently made to Scottish architecture, as represented by the austere stone walls of Huntly Castle (Aberdeenshire, 15th century) or Linlithgow Palace (West Lothian, Scotland, rebuilt 1622). It is the architect's use of heavy masonry, together with his affirmation that Scottish "baronial" architecture was its only real indigenous style, that leads to this conclusion. The Glasgow School of Art is almost bare of the kinds of sculptural or decorative elements that were expected at the time, and remains relatively forbidding in its austerity.

Wrought iron was employed for decorative details, but in keeping with Mackintosh's view that "construction should be decorated, and not decoration constructed." The facades of the building are different but all asymmetrical, as is emphasized in such details as the off-center entrance. Modernity is evident in the use of large, industrial-style windows, amongst other elements. Construction for the main building, located on Renfrew Street, began in 1897.

A second phase built between 1907 and 1909 for financial reasons included a two-story library with a mezzanine. Interiors were designed in collaboration with the architect's wife, Margaret Macdonald, in an often floral or geometric mode with metal and polychrome details. On the whole, the decorative elements do not make it possible to fully affiliate this building with styles like art nouveau. It is eclectic in its forms and references, and in this it retains a degree of modernity that surpasses any period style.

The Glasgow School of Art, founded in 1845, is still Scotland's only independent art school, offering highly regarded university programs in architecture, design, and fine art. As of early 2013, a new building designed by Steven Holl, located opposite the Mackintosh structure that presently houses the Fine Art Painting Department, was under construction. Holl states, "We aim for a building in complementary contrast to Charles Rennie Mackintosh's 1909 Glasgow School of Art—forging a symbiotic relation in which each structure heightens the integral qualities of the other. We envision a thin translucent materiality in considered contrast to the masonry of the Mackintosh building—volumes of light which express the school's activity in the urban fabric embodying a forward-looking life for the arts."

1910

AEG Turbine Factory

BERLIN, GERMANY

THE AEG TURBINE FACTORY in Berlin was designed for the Allgemeine Elektricitäts-Gesesellschaft (German Electricity Company) by Peter Behrens (1868–1940) and the engineer Karl Bernhard and completed in 1910 in Moabit, an area approximately two miles (3 kilometers) from the heart of the German capital. AEG was founded by Emil Rathenau (1838–1915), an industrialist who realized the potential of electrical technology and acquired the rights to manufacture items based on the patents of Thomas Edison in 1881. Rathenau's German Edison Society for Applied Electricity (Deutsche Edison-Gesellschaft für angewandte Elektricität) became AEG in 1887.

The Behrens building is located on the southern edge of their Berlin factory complex. Beginning in 1899, Beherns participated with others such as Joseph Maria Olbrich in the Darmstadt Artists' Colony, where he built his own house. In 1907 Behrens was one of the founders of the Deutscher Werkbund (German Work Federation), an association of artists, architects, designers, and industrialists that emphasized modernity and paved the way for the creation of the Bauhaus. Behrens was in fact hired by AEG in 1907 as an artistic consultant. He designed AEG's corporate identity (logos, product design, advertising, etc.). His role was thus that of fashioning the company's image and giving its industrial goals roots in culture and history.

Behrens created an unembarrassed ode to the industry, calling on Greek and Egyptian temple design in order to glorify the emerging power of electricity. In philosophical terms, he believed in the power of art to transform and dignify everyday life. Rather than glorifying the machine, as some later modern architects did with force, Behrens sought to impose the victory of art over banality. The AEG Turbine Factory was his first industrial building, and it was regarded immediately as an unprecedented break with the immediate past. It presented the challenge of the technical constraints of the use of the structure, such as the internal traveling crane, as opposed to the architect's artistic goals. Although the building has a templelike quality, its central window has a size that was rendered possible only through the use of modern

techniques. The rectangular floor plan of the structure is nearly 680 feet (207 meters) long and an impressive 82 feet (25 meters) wide. Visible steel columns frame large areas of glass.

Behrens himself was not inclined to engineering prowess, so he relied on Karl Bernhard, with whom he had a contentious relationship, for that aspect of the design. Elements such as the crystalline angling of the gable ends of the building are not so much structural as they are an indication that, in the mind of the architect, the workplace had to be a place of dignity.

The architect Erich Mendelsohn was a critic of the project because he felt that the structural reality of the building was disguised by Behrens's need to create a temple of industry. Le Corbusier chose to see the interior, with its "admirable moderation and cleanness, with magnificent machines, which set solemn and impressive accents, as the center of attraction." The nave of the Behrens building was intended for the manufacture of turbines for power generation. Le Corbusier was focusing on the machine aspect of the architecture in his remarks, but Behrens remains his mentor. Le Corbusier, Gropius, and Mies van der Rohe were all at one point assistants or students of Behrens between 1907 and 1912.

1913

Grand Central Terminal

NEW YORK, NEW YORK, UNITED STATES

GRAND CENTRAL TERMINAL in New York opened on February 2, 1913, and was visited by no fewer than 150,000 people on its opening day. The New York Times wrote, "The Grand Central Terminal is not only a station, it is a monument, a civic center, or, if one will, a city. Without exception, it is not only the greatest station in the United States, but the greatest station, of any type, in the world." The use of electricity in place of steam for locomotives allowed the creation of the main concourse, a spectacular space 300 feet (91.4 meters) long, 125 feet (38 meters) wide, and equally high. A four-faced clock surmounting the information booth in the midst of the concourse is one of its most famous features. The ceiling paintings representing a reversed view of the constellations are the work of the French artist Paul César Helleu (1859–1927). Another artistic feature of the terminal is a sculptural group representing Mercury, Hercules, and Minerva by another French artist, Jules-Alexis Coutan.

Circulation within the building was improved over earlier facilities through the separation of inbound and outbound passengers. Located at Forty-second Street, astride Park Avenue, and covering an area of 48 acres (19 hectares), Grand Central was at the time the largest train terminal in the world. It still serves nearly 22 million travelers a year. Aside from numerous shops, restaurants including the well-known Oyster Bar are part of the design. From 1922 to 1958 the terminal was the location of the Grand Central Art Galleries, established by John Singer Sargent and others.

Grand Central Terminal was built on the site of the Grand Central Depot (1871), which was designed by John Snook for Cornelius Vanderbilt. Parts of this structure were demolished near the end of the nineteenth century and tracks were reconfigured, at that time leading the facility to be renamed Grand Central Station. As a result of a serious accident in a rail tunnel at Fifty-eighth Street caused by steam and smoke, steam locomotives were forbidden in New York in 1902. This decision is related to the reconstruction of the entire facility in phases beginning in 1903. The designs by the architects Reed and

Stem of St. Paul, Minnesota, and Warren and Wetmore of New York were put in place at the same time as the electrification of the railways involved progressed. By the 1950s, with the decline in rail travel, it was possible for the developer William Zeckendorf to propose replacing the station with an eighty-story tower, with a design created by I. M. Pei.

The architect Santiago Calatrava, architect of the new World Trade Center Transportation Hub in Manhattan, stated: "The feeling that I get in the main concourse of Grand Central Terminal is that it is the product of great intelligence. It gives a particular sense, even a sacred aspect to commerce. While sacrificing nothing of its utility, the station becomes an act of celebration. Look at all that has sprung up around the void at the heart of Grand Central—the Seagram Building and Park Avenue itself. In America no building resembles the Pantheon so closely in these terms. Look at what the architects have placed in the center of the great hall—a clock and a small stand intended to give away timetables—two elements intended to give rather than to take from travelers. We need beauty, and beauty can generate great things."

Grand Central Terminal
New York, New York,
United States, 1913

(ABOVE)
Exterior of Grand Central
Terminal from 42nd Street.

(RIGHT)
The Express Concourse of
Grand Central Terminal.

1925

Bauhaus

DESSAU, GERMANY

IN 1919 THE SCHOOLS of art and applied arts of the grand duchy of Saxony were combined to form the State Bauhaus of Weimar, which was housed in buildings designed by Henry van de Velde (1863–1957) and completed in 1904 and 1911. From the first, the goal of the Bauhaus was to create what was called a *Gesamtkunstwerk* (total work of art) in which all arts, including architecture, would be brought together. According to the Bauhaus manifesto (1919), "The building is the ultimate goal of all fine art." Such famous artists as Lyonel Feininger, Oskar Schlemmer, Paul Klee, Wassily Kandinsky, and Theo van Doesburg participated in the Bauhaus as well. Just as the Bauhaus can be related to the earlier Werkbund founded amongst others by Peter Behrens in 1907, the German organization may be compared to Vkhutemas, the Russian state art and technical school founded in 1920 in Moscow.

The Bauhaus sought in 1924 to leave Weimar because of political conflicts. The decision was made to create a school in the city of Dessau, located 75 miles (120 kilometers) south of Berlin. Bauhaus director Walter Gropius designed a new three-story workshop, a school block, and a five-story structure containing 28 studios (1925–26, with Ernst Neufert and Carl Fieger, both from his own office), built with the assistance of the city. A glass curtain wall was used to create an impression of lightness and to render the structural elements visible. Connecting blocks are also part of the design: the Festive Area connecting the studios and workshop area, and a bridge between the school and the workshop. Gropius set up his own office in this bridge, where it remained until 1928.

As seen in the plan, the Bauhaus Dessau evokes a pinwheel shape that is apparently related to the airplane propellers that were manufactured at the time in the region. The architecture was thus not abstract but rather figurative, in a new, mechanical sense. The reinforced concrete and brickwork structures at Dessau had asphalt roofs that could be walked on. Fully conscious of modernity in all its forms, Gropius stated, "With the development of air transport, the architect will have to pay as

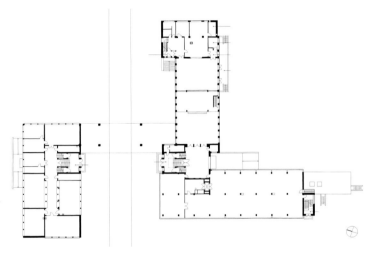

much attention to the bird's-eye perspective of his houses as to their elevations."

Gropius was succeeded in 1928 by Hannes Meyer and then from 1930 to 1933 by Ludwig Mies van der Rohe. Closed down by the authorities in Dessau on September 30, 1932, the school moved briefly to Berlin in an old factory building rehabilitated by Mies for use by the Bauhaus during an eleven-month period beginning in late 1932. The following year, the Gestapo closed down the "degenerate" operation. Both Gropius and Mies van der Rohe of course went on to have considerable influence on teaching and architecture in the United States. The Dessau complex was damaged during the war and used by the East German government as a design and architecture school beginning in 1976. Restored in that same year, the building now houses the Bauhaus Dessau Foundation.

The Bauhaus sites in Weimar and Dessau were included on the UNESCO World Heritage List in 1996. The international organization considered that the site is of "outstanding universal value" since these buildings are the "seminal works of the Bauhaus architectural school, the foundation of the Modern Movement which was to revolutionize artistic and architectural thinking and practice in the twentieth century." The Dessau building by Gropius was actually a central element in UNESCO's vote to include the Bauhaus sites in its list.

1932

Chrysler Building

NEW YORK, NEW YORK, UNITED STATES

THE CHRYSLER BUILDING, located on Lexington Avenue at Forty-second Street in Manhattan, was built between 1928 and 1932. It was briefly the tallest building in the world, surpassing the Eiffel Tower in Paris at seventy-seven stories and 1,047 feet (319 meters) in height. In fact, the uppermost levels of the tower are used mostly for access and broadcasting equipment. Renzo Piano's New York Times building was topped out at the same height in 2007. Built for Walter Chrysler, it housed the headquarters of the carmaker until the 1950s. It was designed by William Van Alen (1883–1954), who studied architecture in Paris under Victor Laloux. The relationship between client and architect was acrimonious at the end, with a lawsuit pitting one against the other over the architect's fees.

Though it has a steel frame, the building's walls were actually made with hand-laid bricks, with metal cladding on the exterior. An interesting aspect of the construction is that, with New York engaged in a race to build the world's tallest building, William Van Alen secretly planned the addition of a spire to his tower. He was under instructions from the client to make the building the tallest in the world, and a rival architect, H. Craig Severance, was seeking to go even higher with his Bank of Manhattan Company tower on Wall Street. The construction itself, which employed up to three thousand workers at a time, allowed the addition of up to four floors a week to the tower. The 125 foot (38 meter) metal tip was put in place in just ninety minutes on October 23, 1929, allowing the Chrysler Building to be the tallest skyscraper, only to be surpassed less than a year later by the Empire State Building, at Thirty-fourth Street and Fifth Avenue. Significantly, the spire also made the Chrysler Building the first structure to be taller than 1,000 feet (305 meters).

Despite its still-modern appearance, the Chrysler Building has a number of decorative details, such as ornaments inspired by the form of the silver-winged radiator caps designed in 1924 by Oliver Clark for the Chrysler Six, or large metal eagles perched at the corners of the sixty-first floor. The stainless steel top of the building remains its most distinctive feature, but other elements, such as the lobby, clad in marble, onyx, and amber, affirm the adherence to the art deco style. Somewhat difficult to define, art deco, which originated in France, was something of a rejection of the organic forms of art nouveau. The Chrysler Building's successive radiating stainless steel sunburst patterns near its top are cited as an exemplary development of the style in skyscraper design, as are the Egyptian patterns inside. The extensive use of metal in the building's facade was also considered innovative at the time.

The New York property developer William Zeckendorf bought the building in 1953 from the Chrysler family, with the actual site belonging to the Cooper Union, a New York college. Since 2008, the Abu Dhabi Investment Council has owned most of the tower. It remains one of the favorite skyscrapers of both architects and New Yorkers, an unusual indicator of lasting success.

1938

Fallingwater

MILL RUN, PENNSYLVANIA, UNITED STATES

FALLINGWATER, the Edgar J. Kaufmann House, built between 1936 and 1938, may be the most famous house of the twentieth century. Surprisingly, even before it was finished, it had been published throughout the world—a drawing for the house appears in the background of Wright's portrait on the cover of *Time* magazine in January 1938. That same month, photographs were exhibited at the Museum of Modern Art in New York and then published in *Architectural Forum*. Despite an occasionally stormy relationship, Wright's success in this instance owes much to his client, the owner of a Pittsburgh department store who came to be known locally as "the merchant prince." At the age of sixty-nine, Wright was witnessing a career that seemed to have come to an end, but Fallingwater revived his fortunes.

Although the Kaufmann family commissioned Wright for roughly a dozen projects between 1934 and the architect's death, only three—Fallingwater, its guesthouse, and Edgar Kaufmann's private office in the department store—were realized. (This office can now be seen at the Victoria and Albert Museum in London.) In 1946, Kaufmann asked Richard Neutra to design a house for him in Palm Springs, California. Incensed by what he felt was infidelity, Wright broke off relations with Kaufmann, only to reconcile with his client shortly thereafter. The Kaufmann House in Palm Springs, rendered almost equally famous by the 1947 photographs by Julius Schulman, is another icon of twentieth-century American architecture.

Fallingwater has a floor area of 5,330 square feet (495 square meters), of which 2,885 square feet (268 square meters) are interior space, and 2,445 square feet (227 square meters) are terraces. The architect used only two colors of paint for the house: a light ochre for the concrete and his signature Cherokee red for the steel. The house opened to the public in 1964, and it received more than 160,000 visitors in 2011.

Much has been written about Frank Lloyd Wright's organic approach to architecture and, indeed, to Fallingwater in particular. The audacity of designing a house directly over a waterfall and using its massing and design to make the site into something more than it was naturally are hallmarks of Wright's style and genius. "I think nature should be spelled with a capital N,"

he said, "not because nature is God but because all that we can learn of God we will learn from the body of God, which we call nature." This interesting remark does a good deal to explain an attitude that consists in imagining the architect's role as being one of "improving" on nature and, surely, not one of imitation. As William Cronon wrote in the catalogue of the Museum of Modern Art's 1994 exhibition on the architect, "For Wright, the purpose of art and architecture was not slavishly to copy external nature, but to use it in the way Emerson recommended, as the occasion for exploring inner nature and thereby expressing universal spirit."

There is an undeniable grandeur in the way Fallingwater sits above the rocks and transforms the natural setting, a mastery that few modern architects other than Wright have displayed. The mixture of stone walls and cantilevered, reinforced concrete slabs at once ties the residence to nature and yet makes it into a truly modern house.

Fallingwater
Mill Run, Pennsylvania,
United States, 1938

(ABOVE)
Frank Lloyd Wright designed
the furniture and interiors to
complement his architectural
design. The dining table and
bookshelves appear to echo the
cantilever of the structure and
contrast smooth dark wood with
the rough texture of the
stonework.

(RIGHT)
The sound of running water
permeates every room of
Fallingwater. The open stairs
descend from a hatchway in the
living room to provide a direct
connection with the stream.

1954

Notre Dame du Haut

RONCHAMP, FRANCE

COMMISSIONED BY THE Association de l'Oeuvre Notre Dame du Haut (Association for the Works of Notre Dame du Haut), Le Corbusier's most famous church was completed in 1954. The concrete and stone structure with an upturned roof comprises three chapels, a main altar, and two side entrances. It was built on a hilltop site in eastern France, where Christian chapels have existed since the fourth century. In an unusual gesture for such a modern architect, Le Corbusier used the stones of the earlier chapel destroyed during the Second World War to fill the thick southern wall of Notre Dame du Haut, thus giving the new structure an affiliation with the past that went beyond its site. As he was in the later project of Sainte Marie de La Tourette in Lyon, (1960), the Dominican friar Marie-Alain Couturier was a driving force behind this project.

Structurally, the chapel has a number of unexpected features. One of these is the unusual curved roof that appears almost to float above the walls. Indeed, this thick concrete shell roof is supported by concrete columns rather than by the walls. An opening at the top of the walls allows light into the space, while the floor of the chapel slopes downward in the direction of the white stone altar, in keeping with the inclined terrain. All these features are unusual in terms of the more purely geometric vocabulary normally used by the architect.

The southern wall of the chapel, in some places as thick as ten feet (3 meters), is marked by irregular windows, some of which have abstract stained-glass designs, allowing a variety of different colors of light to fill the interior. Many surfaces of the walls are finished in sprayed concrete (Gunite) that was whitewashed. The architect also created furnishings for the structure, including an unexpected outdoor altar. In April 2012, Michael Kimmelman wrote for the *New York Times* that "what Le Corbusier called the chapel's 'ineffable space' derives not from Zen-like simplicity or Baroque extravagance but from

this quasi-Cubist asymmetry of robust, jaunty, sensuous shapes, held in improbable equilibrium as if by a juggler on a tightrope. It's a sculptural feat."

In 2011, a new building by Renzo Piano was inaugurated just 300 feet (91 meters) from Le Corbusier's monument of modern architecture. The visitor center and convent was cut into the hillside in order to avoid any conflict with the earlier building. Piano's building, with its simple clean lines formed with concrete, zinc, and wood, was the object of conflicting petitions involving some of the best-known architects in the world when the project was announced. The petition against the project, addressed to France's minister of culture, was signed by numerous architects including Rafael Moneo, Richard Meier, and Cesar Pelli. An online petition in support of the project drew the support of Massimiliano Fuksas, David Adjaye, Tadao Ando, and John Pawson, amongst others. The new buildings are an oratory of 9,688 square feet (900 square meters), an array of nuns' cells of equal area with small gardens, and the 4,800 square foot (446 square meter) visitor center.

1958

Seagram Building

NEW YORK, NEW YORK, UNITED STATES

DESPITE A NUMBER OF iconic towers in major cities all over the world, few manage to resist the passage of time in terms of their design. The Seagram Building, located at 375 Park Avenue, between Fifty-second and Fifty-third Streets in Manhattan, is an obvious exception to this rule. It was designed by Ludwig Mies van der Rohe, in collaboration with Philip Johnson, for the Canadian firm Joseph E. Seagram's and Sons. The thirty-eight-story structure is 516 feet (157.3 meters) tall and was completed in 1958.

Contrary to numerous towers whose number of stories and structure are hidden behind full glass-curtain walls, the bronze-colored frame of the Seagram tower is entirely visible. Though the tower does have a dark appearance on the whole, its bronze notes and window coloring give it a golden hue in the final analysis, a kind of ethereal cladding that was born of careful calculation and aesthetic sense. With its extreme regularity, the building surely fits well into the modernist ethos of Mies van der Rohe and other heirs of Germany's Bauhaus, but in this instance, the structure also assumes a classical elegance that escapes no one who takes the time to view its design.

The visual unity of the tower is reinforced by the architect's insistence that window blinds should function only in certain predetermined positions. In fact, the beams employed on the facades suggest the actual structure but do not support the weight of the building. The steel frame structure has a steel and reinforced concrete core. Making use of no less than fifteen hundred tons of bronze, the moderately sized skyscraper was reputed to have been the most expensive building in the world when it was completed, a title usurped in 1986 by Norman Foster's Hong Kong and Shanghai Bank, followed by others. With its granite plaza, designed in the same strict rectilinear spirit as the tower itself, the Seagram Building, together with Lever House (Skidmore Owings Merrill, 1954) located on the opposite side of Park Avenue, had a great influence on New York architecture, and, surely, that of many other cities as well.

The Seagram Building is set no less than 100 feet (30 meters) from Park Avenue, a civic gesture that the city of New York encouraged, but which makes the street more convivial at this point than anywhere buildings are aligned on the required sidewalks. The architect Philip Johnson designed office spaces in the tower, but also the Four Seasons restaurant, whose entrance is at the lower street level on Fifty-second Street. On the Fifty-third Street side, the Brasserie restaurant caters to those with slightly lower budgets but retains a sense of modern style, updated by the architects Diller and Scofidio in 1999. The broad stair of the Four Seasons leads to a bar, followed by a high passageway entirely glazed on one side that opens into the grand dining room, one of New York's most celebrated interior spaces. Shimmering curtains reveal glimpses of the surrounding towers, while a central white marble fountain brings to mind a kind of modern classicism that Johnson correctly interpreted as being the ultimate goal of Mies van der Rohe.

1958

Palace of the Dawn

BRASÍLIA, BRAZIL

I T IS CALLED THE PALACE of the Dawn (Palácio da Alvorada), and it was one of the first buildings to rise from the nearly empty plain of what was to become Brasília. Often published yet rarely visited because it is the residence of the presidents of Brazil, as its name implies, the Palace of the Dawn faces the rising sun. Sitting alone at the end of a broad expanse of grass, it appears to float on shallow basins, its unusual curved columns scarcely touching the ground. The 75,347 square foot (7,000 square meter) structure is located near the artificial Paranoá Lake. Construction began on April 3, 1957. Though its weightlessness is partly illusory because of hidden supports, the Palace of the Dawn is in truth a remarkable feat of architecture and engineering. Oscar Niemeyer collaborated closely with the engineer Joachim Cardoso to approach the utmost limits of structural feasibility in the pursuit of ideal proportions and lightness. Niemeyer continually challenged the limits of concrete architecture, in part thanks to the engineers like Cardoso who were his faithful collaborators.

A rectangular glass prism hovering between thin slabs of concrete, the palace has two floors devoted respectively to official receptions and to the living space of the president. Great sliding glass doors open into a high airy space where light and modernity rule. To imagine that the charismatic president of Brazil, Juscelino Kubitschek, inaugurated this residence hardly a year later, on June 30, 1958, is to take the measure of the open spirits who gave birth to the new capital. It was Kubitschek himself who inspired the name of this palace when he asked, "What is Brasília, if not the dawn of a new day for Brazil?" A gold-colored wall in the entrance to the palace inscribed with a quote by Kubitschek further emphasizes the relation between the idea of a new dawn and the rising architecture of the new capital: "From this central plateau, this vast loneliness that will soon become

the center of national decisions, I look once more at the future of my country and foresee this dawn with an unshakeable faith in its great destiny."

A small chapel, whose spiral form reveals an inspirational economy of means, accompanies the main structure of the palace. Again, the expected rectilinear pattern is broken in order to achieve an uplifting lightness. Here, as in so many of his projects, Niemeyer called on artists, in this case Maria Martins and Alfredo Ceschiatti, to provide a counterpoint to the largely abstract vocabulary of his architecture. Well cared for as befits its function, superbly isolated in ample grounds, the Palácio da Alvorada seems to exist in a state of suspended, surreal perfection, hovering between earth and sky. The Palace of the Dawn was restored between 2004 and 2006. Even today, there is an elegance and grace about this building that belies its construction more than fifty years ago. It remains thoroughly modern and inventive, a symbol of which Brazil can be proud and proof that Oscar Niemeyer was indeed one of the greatest architects of the twentieth century.

Palace of the Dawn
Brasília, Brazil, 1958

(ABOVE)
The entrance hall of the
official residence of the
Presidents of Brazil.

(RIGHT)
The composition includes
a small chapel on the left
accenting the horizontal
lines of the palace.

1962

TWA Flight Center

QUEENS, NEW YORK, UNITED STATES

THE TWA FLIGHT CENTER was designed by the architect Eero Saarinen. It opened at Idlewild (now John F. Kennedy International) Airport in 1962. Justifiably celebrated for its lyrical modernism, the structure was openly inspired by the image of a bird in flight. This metaphorical reference was created by a thin-shell roof arching over the passenger spaces and allowing for ample glazing. Conceived as the epitome of modernity at the time, the terminal featured a central public address system and other such innovations as baggage carousels and an electronic departure board. With hardly a straight line in its design, the TWA Flight Center also represented a concerted effort on the part of the architect to control an entire public environment—inside and out. Saarinen stated, "All the curves, all the spaces and elements right down to the shape of the signs, display boards, railings and check-in desks were to be of a matching nature. We wanted passengers passing through the building to experience a fully designed environment, in which each part arises from another and everything belongs to the same formal world."

The terminal is now used by the JetBlue Airways Corporation. Though calls for the modernization of the airport have in the past led to calls for the demolition of the building, it was designated a historic landmark by the city of New York in 1994. Saarinen received the commission in 1956, but the architect did not live to see the opening of the terminal in May 1962. A lounge and passenger area were added by Kevin Roche in 1969.

A number of well-known American architects, including Philip Johnson and Robert Stern, have defended the original structure and sometimes spoken out against proposed changes. Johnson in particular sought to avoid having other structures built in the areas that allow passengers to see the sky from the interior of the pavilion. Not used from 2001 to 2004, the TWA building did see a large new structure added beginning in 2005; it was completed in 2008 by the large architectural firm Gensler. JetBlue reopened the enlarged facility in 2008, with the promise of creating an aviation museum and conference center in the older structure. One obvious difficulty of the original terminal was that it relied on methods that changed with the advent of high-capacity aircraft and security issues, particularly after the events of September 11, 2001. The building, a stand-alone monument to air travel, was simply not made to be updated in an appropriate way. However, it did anticipate a certain number of signature buildings, such as Kansai International Airport in Osaka, Japan (Renzo Piano; 1994), that have succeeded it in an effort to create architecture that is symbolic of the excitement of air travel. It is true that the emphatic wing design of the TWA Flight Center is more emblematic of its time, the 1960s, than it might be of the present, even if certain architects like Santiago Calatrava find the image of a bird taking flight to be a legitimate source of inspiration for contemporary work.

1965

Salk Institute

LA JOLLA, CALIFORNIA, UNITED STATES

Louis I. Kahn was born in 1901 in Kingisepp, on the island of Ösel in Estonia. His family moved to Philadelphia in 1906, and he became a naturalized U.S. citizen in 1915. He had completed the Yale Art Gallery (1951–53) in New Haven, Connecticut, prior to the Salk Institute for Biological Studies (1959–65) in La Jolla, California. The Salk Institute was established in the 1960s by Jonas Salk, the developer of the polio vaccine. He wanted to make it possible for biologists and others to work together "in a collaborative environment that would encourage them to consider the wider implications of their discoveries for the future of humanity." Salk was closely involved with the architect in the design. He stated that his goal was to "create a facility worthy of a visit by Picasso." In 1960, the city of San Diego approved a gift of land for the nonprofit Salk Institute on Torrey Pines Mesa, overlooking the ocean. Construction began in 1962 with the assurance that the March of Dimes would provide initial funding for the project.

The original complex is made up of two symmetric buildings with a travertine marble plaza and a narrow watercourse that separates the structures, which have six stories—three floors of laboratories and three levels above that provide "access to utilities." Towers protrude into the courtyard, with those on the west offering six floors of professorial offices looking out onto the Pacific. Concrete for the buildings was made with volcanic ash, which gives it a warm tone ("pozzuolanic" concrete), and the architect stipulated that there was not to be any grinding or painting of the concrete. Aside from the basic concrete structure, only teak, lead, glass, and steel were used. The laboratories of the institute were designed without separating walls in order to encourage collaboration. On the whole, the complex was designed as a kind of intellectual retreat for exceptional figures of modern science.

The Salk Institute is currently involved in molecular biology and genetics, neurosciences, and plant biology. Research focuses

on cancer, diabetes, birth defects, Alzheimer's disease, Parkinson's disease, and AIDS. The original buildings of the Salk Institute were designated as a historical landmark in 1991. In 1992, the Salk Institute received a 25-Year Award from the American Institute of Architects (AIA) and was included in the AIA exhibit "Structures of Our Time: 31 Buildings That Changed Modern Life," with photos by Carol Highsmith. Those who have seen the central court of the Salk Institute and its band of water stretching out toward the Pacific have no doubt about the beauty nor the spirituality of this architecture.

Louis Kahn originally designed other parts for the complex, which were to include a conference building and living quarters, but those schemes were not carried out. Jonas Salk did decide in 1989 to expand the institute, and he hired two architects (Anshen & Allen) who had worked on the original design with Kahn, who died in 1974. Salk made it clear that the Louis Kahn building was not to be altered and that the new wing would be built at some distance from the original structure. The additional laboratories and offices were completed in 1996, receiving a mixed reception just after the death of Jonas Salk.

1973

Sydney Opera House

SYDNEY, AUSTRALIA

IN ADDING THE Sydney Opera House to its World Heritage List in 2007, UNESCO stated, "The Sydney Opera House constitutes a masterpiece of 20th century architecture. Its significance is based on its unparalleled design and construction; its exceptional engineering achievements and technological innovation and its position as a world-famous icon of architecture. It is a daring and visionary experiment that has had an enduring influence on the emergent architecture of the late 20th century."

In 1956, the government of New South Wales organized an open international competition for the project, to be located on Bennelong Point, near the iconic Sydney Harbour Bridge. The winner of the competition was the Danish architect Jørn Utzon. Born in 1918 in Copenhagen, Utzon was relatively unknown when his victory was announced. He worked for a time in Finland with Alvar Aalto and was influenced by Gunnar Asplund. During travel in the United States in 1949, Utzon met Ludwig Mies van der Rohe, Richard Neutra, and Charles and Ray Eames. He created his own office in Copenhagen in 1950.

It is said that Utzon's entry for the Sydney competition was rescued from the rejected projects by jury member and architect Eero Saarinen, who would later be the author of the TWA Flight Center in New York. The distinctive roof shape designed by Utzon was related to his study of naval charts of Sydney Harbor and a personal knowledge of shipbuilding. Construction began in 1959, although the design of the building's shells that cover two halls was refined in an ongoing process of collaboration between the architect and the engineer Ove Arup. At the time of the competition, neither Utzon nor the jury consulted a structural engineer. Precast rib vaults were put in place beginning in 1964. The concrete shells are a series of sections of spheres with a radius of 247 feet (75.2 meters). The whole structure is set on a large podium built on deep concrete piers. It is 607 feet (185 meters) long and 394 feet (120 meters) wide.

A change of government in New South Wales led to the resignation of Utzon in 1966. The glass walls of the Sydney Opera

House and its interiors were then designed by Peter Hall, Lionel Todd, and David Littlemore, together with the New South Wales government architect Ted Farmer. Queen Elizabeth II inaugurated the opera house on October 20, 1973. Utzon was not present, although he was awarded the gold medal of the Royal Institute of Architects.

Utzon again became involved from a distance in schemes to refurbish the building in 1999, leading to the creation of the Utzon Room (2004), the only interior space designed by the architect. Any number of architects have commented on the Sydney Opera House, but the words of Louis Kahn seem most appropriate: "The sun did not know how beautiful its light was, until it was reflected off this building." Utzon won the 2003 Pritzker Prize and died in 2008, never having returned to Australia nor seen his masterwork in its completed form. The Sydney Opera House today conducts three thousand events per year and has an annual attendance of two million for the performances.

Sydney Opera House
Sydney, Australia, 1973

(ABOVE)
Unlike contemporary curvilinear buildings, the complex concrete shells of the Sydney Opera House were designed without the aid of a computer.

(RIGHT)
The Sydney Opera House's signature "sails" of pre-cast concrete formed with permanent ceramic surface tiles rise above the Sydney Harbour Bridge.

1977

Centre Georges Pompidou

PARIS, FRANCE

THE GEORGES POMPIDOU CENTER is in many ways a
seminal structure, not only in the career of Renzo
Piano, but also for the architecture of its time.
Intended as a showcase for modern French culture in the spirit
of President Pompidou, who also encouraged such urban experi-
ments as the towers in the Front de Seine area, the Paris facility
was the result of André Malraux's *maison de la culture* concept,
which posited the concept of culture for everyone. From the
first, the Centre Pompidou embraced various disciplines and
forms of expression, ranging from a library to the National
Museum of Modern Art. Significantly, the engineer Jean Prouvé
was a member of the jury that selected the young team of Renzo
Piano and Richard Rogers. Prouvé's own Maison du Peuple in
Clichy (1939) has been cited as a precursor of the concept of spatial flexibility so important to the Pompidou project. With the
assistance of the engineers Peter Rice and Tom Barker, the structure took real form. Six stories high, with a clear span of 157.5 feet
(48 meters), the Centre stands out near the old Marais district of
Paris as an ode to technically oriented architecture, with its web
of tubular ducts on the east facade and the signature glass escala-
tor, snaking up the 544.6 foot (166 meter) wide west face.

The original Centre included the underground facilities of the
IRCAM, a contemporary music complex headed by Pierre Boulez.
In 1988–90, Piano added a new aboveground structure for the
IRCAM, just across the street from the Centre Pompidou. Its com-
posite brick facade makes it clear that by that time the architect
had set aside the Archigram-style complexity that characterized the
main building. Another small addition to the Centre, the Brancusi
atelier, was added in 1997. Brancusi left numerous sculptures to
the French government on the condition that they remain in his
atelier. The officials of the Centre and Piano approached this condition with a unique combination of modern architecture and a
faithful reconstruction of the original studio on the plateau in front

of Beaubourg. Returning to the Pompidou Center to oversee its
renovation in the late 1990s, Piano cleared the structure of the
overly fussy additions brought to the interiors by other designers
and gave it back a good measure of the transparency and openness
with which it had been designed. Significantly, it could also be said
that his renovation calmed the discordant assemblage of mechanical forms that had characterized the galleries and other interior
public spaces from 1977 on.

The Centre Pompidou, with its year-in-year-out average of
nearly twenty thousand visitors per day, is one of the most visited
monuments in Europe. Granted, many are more attracted to the
view of Paris from the uppermost level than by modern art, yet
the public acceptance of the building has made it a lasting witness
to the "triumph" of modern architecture in the still traditionally
oriented environment of many of Europe's old cities. Both Renzo
Piano and Richard Rogers went on to have brilliant careers in part
as a result of their selection to design this building.

1989

Church of the Light

IBARAKI, OSAKA, JAPAN

ONE OF THE BEST-KNOWN works by the Japanese architect Tadao Ando, this project retains all of the strength and freshness that it had at the time of its opening. The original church has since been augmented by an adjoining Sunday School (1999), also designed by Ando. With an area of just 1,216 square feet (113 square meters), built for the Ibaraki Kasugaoka church, a member of the United Church of Christ in Japan, at the behest of the Reverend Noboru Karukome, it is an expression of the power that contemporary architecture can convey in the hands of a master such as Ando.

Like all of Ando's buildings, particularly those in Japan, the thick concrete walls of the Church of the Light have a "softness" that belies their rough origins. Essentially a rectangular concrete box intersected at a fifteen-degree angle by a freestanding wall, the chapel's most remarkable feature is the cruciform opening behind the altar, which floods the interior with light. With floors and pews made of blackened cedar scaffolding planks, the interior projects an image of simplicity that is confirmed by the unusual downward-sloping floor. For Reverend Karukome, the fact that the altar is set at the lowest point of the church symbolized "Jesus Christ who came down to the lowest of us all."

Ando says that he would have preferred to leave the glass out of the cross-shaped opening, allowing the wind to enter just as the light does, but climatic conditions in winter rendered this solution unacceptable to the church officials. As is usually the case, the cross imagined by Ando is not quite a Christian one—the cross bar is too low for that direct interpretation—and yet there can be little doubt what parishioners see inside the relatively dark space. When describing this project, the architect refers to a "quest for the relation between light and shadow" and the need for a "shelter for the spirit." The second phase of the project included an assembly hall, a kitchen, and a library space. The structure "consists of a rectangular parallelepiped made of concrete, embracing a double-height void, sliced through at a 15-degree angle by an oblique wall." Japanese linden plywood boards are integrated into the architecture, and the furniture is almost entirely designed by Ando.

Despite the use of plywood, the Sunday School does have a slightly more sophisticated or "polished" aspect than that of its predecessor. With a floor area of 1,604 square feet (149 square meters), the school is larger than the church, but it is a testimony to the architect's subtlety that it neither overwhelms nor denatures the first structure. The penetration of an oblique wall at a fifteen-degree angle obviously echoes the design of the church, but in this composition, it is the spatial variety of the new building that strikes the visitor more than any repetition. Ando has also created a small canopy-covered seating area linking the two structures. The site is relatively tight, a fact that in no way detracts from the success and power of the work.

1983–98

The Grand Louvre

PARIS, FRANCE

IN 1989, I. M. PEI stated, "The Grand Louvre will hold the first place in my life as an architect." To the casual observer, this might seem a surprising statement. The only part of Pei's work visible from the exterior of the palace is a glass pyramid and a square around it, the Cour Napoléon. But the Louvre is more than a museum or a former royal residence. Pei's Grand Louvre project concerned nothing other than the historic heart of the history of France. Though controversy greeted the first announcement of the pyramid, the architect convinced the French president François Mitterrand, museum authorities, and then the country at large that his vision was the correct one to bring the Louvre into the twentieth century. Indeed, Mitterrand's Grands Travaux, essentially located in the French capital, were meant to emphasize the central role of culture in the country. Geographically set between Jean Nouvel's Institut du Monde Arabe at one side of the city and the Arche de la Défense (Johan Otto van Sprekelsen and Paul Andreu) on the other, the Louvre, beyond its place as a museum, was without a doubt a vital element of government policy, a key to understanding the evolution of modern France. Today, the pyramid has become as much a symbol of Paris as the Eiffel Tower.

The history of the Louvre as a place for the display of art began before the end of the seventeenth century to the extent that the Royal Academy of Painting and Sculpture (Académie Royale de Peinture et de Sculpture) exhibited in the Grande Galerie for the first time in 1699. The Museum Central des Arts opened there on August 10, 1793. Until the 1980s, parts of the Louvre were occupied by the French Ministry of the Economy. On September 26, 1981, within four months of his election, Mitterrand announced that the whole palace would become a museum. Pei's careful examination of the building and its history led him to conclude that digging into the Cour Napoléon was the only solution. A central entrance would thus be created, partially solving the difficulties raised by the very large scale of the structures and the distance between the long wings along the Seine on one side and the rue de Rivoli on the other. In line

with the president's announcement concerning the use of the entire palace by the museum, Pei's scheme depended in part on the refurbishment of the Richelieu Wing, at that time still occupied by the Ministry of the Economy.

The Grand Louvre project lasted a total of fifteen years, from 1983 to 1998. It concerned a site area of 22 acres (8.9 hectares). In the first phase involving the pyramid, the square around it, and the larger underground spaces, including a new public entrance, shops, restaurants, temporary exhibition galleries, and much-needed "backstage" space (construction 1984–89), a total of 667,254 square feet (61,990 square meters) of space was added to the Louvre. Also included in the first phase was work related to the discovery of substantial archeological elements, in particular in the Cour Carrée, which were restored and integrated into an underground presentation of the history of the palace. In the second phase (construction 1989–93), the Richelieu Wing of the palace became part of the museum, with a further 538,000 square feet (49,982 square meters) of demolition, followed by new construction within the preserved walls of the palace.

The Grand Louvre
Paris, France, 1983–98

(RIGHT)
The glass pyramid marks the
new entrance to the museum.

1994

Kansai International Airport Terminal

OSAKA, JAPAN

ONE OF THE LARGEST ARCHITECTURAL and engineering undertakings of the late twentieth century, Kansai International Airport was built on a 1,263 acre (511 hectare) artificial island located in the Bay of Osaka. Renzo Piano was selected from a prestigious field in an international competition in 1988. The unusual curved shape of the 1.06 mile (1.7 kilometer) main terminal building is related to the need of air traffic control to maintain visual contact with taxiing aircraft at all times. Piano used this formal constraint to the benefit of his design, making reference to works of art such as Brancusi's *Bird in Space* as well as aircraft or gliders. It will not escape visitors' notice that the dramatically curved roof also recalls a wave pattern for this island airport. The curve of the terminal was in fact conceived as a small section of an imaginary torus 20.4 miles (32.8 kilometers) in diameter, whose main volume would be underground. With its 272.3 foot (83 meter) long arches on the upper floor, the terminal offers a real feeling of freedom to travelers. Rail transfer to nearby cities such as Osaka or Kyoto is easy, as is high-speed boat travel to Kobe and other destinations.

The construction of such a large building on an artificial island in an area with high seismic activity posed many technical problems; these were solved in good part with the assistance of Ove Arup & Partners using a system of hydraulic joints designed to compensate for the predicted settling of the landfill. The seismic resistance of the structure was clearly proven on the occasion of the so-called Great Hanshin Earthquake (N 34.36° E 135.03°) on January 17, 1995. Kansai Airport suffered no damage, not even broken glass, although it is located as close to the epicenter of the earthquake as Kobe. This earthquake (7.2 on the Richter scale) left 5,480 dead, 236,000 homeless, and more than 67,000 homes completely destroyed, principally in Kobe.

Although its visible interior structure may, under some angles, recall the forms of the Pompidou Center, Kansai Airport has a flowing ease in its design that was certainly born of Piano's experience. Simply put, the traveler finds his way easily in this airport

and, even more important, feels comfortable at all times. Seen from the air, the 82,000 stainless steel panels covering the 968,752 square foot (90,000 square meter) roof often shine in the sun, offering a more congenial image than most other airports.

Renzo Piano's own description of the project is also of interest: "We investigated streams of air, from which the form of the terminal's roof would emerge. In cross section, the roof is an irregular arch (in reality a series of arches of different radii), given this shape to channel air from the passenger side of the terminal to the runway side without the need for closed ducts. Baffles left open to view guide the airflow along the ceiling and reflect the light coming from above. We were creating an aerodynamic ceiling, concerned not with the flow of air outside, but inside. Kansai is a precision instrument, a child of mathematics and technology. It forms a strong and recognizable landmark; it has a clear and simple shape that declares itself without hesitation. It is a structure with undulating, asymmetrical lines. It spreads over the island like a glider—a missing link between ground and airplane."

1997

Guggenheim Bilbao

BILBAO, SPAIN

THOMAS KRENS, the director of the Solomon R. Guggenheim Foundation in the 1990s, was very clear about the ambitions he had for the architecture of the Guggenheim Bilbao. He wanted a building equivalent in impact to the Sydney Opera House or to the Centre Pompidou in Paris. He wanted nothing less than an architectural triumph comparable to the Cathedral of Chartres. It may be too early to judge its durability, but Frank Gehry's great titanium vessel, moored to the banks of the Nervión River in the heart of industrial Bilbao, is considered one of the most important buildings of the late twentieth century. The architect Philip Johnson did not hesitate to call it "the greatest building of our time." The museum is one of Gehry's most spectacular architectural works.

Located on the Bay of Biscay, Bilbao is the fourth largest city in Spain, a port, and a manufacturing center. Gehry's project was in fact part of a larger urban renewal effort undertaken by Basque authorities beginning in the late 1980s, with the collaboration of such architects as Norman Foster, Santiago Calatrava, Rafael Moneo, and Arata Isozaki. The building is located on the Nervión River. Its largest gallery is crossed over by the Puente de La Salve, one of the main vehicular entrances to the city. Though it has been said that the Guggenheim Bilbao makes reference in its atrium to Frank Lloyd Wright's Guggenheim Museum on Fifth Avenue in New York, it most of all brings to mind a great shining ship, anchored in the midst of a former port that had seen better days. It is an exceptional success story in terms of bringing an old industrial town back to life with culture.

Groundbreaking for the Guggenheim Bilbao occurred in 1993, and it opened to the public on October 19, 1997. The structure has total floor space of 78,740 square feet (24,000 square meters), with 24,776 square feet (10,600 square meters) of exhibition area on three levels. From the outside, its most spectacular feature is the titanium cladding of its "metallic flower" shapes, which were modeled by Gehry using the CATIA

program developed by Dassault Aviation in France for fighter plane design. On the inside, visitors are greeted by a 180 foot (55 meter) high atrium that cuts through the heart of the building. There are eighteen galleries, but by far the most spectacular of these is the main exhibition space, which is free of structural columns and measures no less than 427 feet (130 meters) in length and 98 feet (30 meters) in width. Inevitably, such spaces do invite comparison to the cathedrals of another era. Gehry also reaches the apogee here of his natural tendency to want to create buildings that are in and of themselves works of art. It seems unexpected that an architect with the inventive capacity of Gehry should build his real masterpiece so far from the "anything goes" climes of Southern California. This has to do with the persuasive powers of Thomas Krens, but also with the maturity of the Guggenheim Bilbao as a piece of architectural art in and of itself. In many ways, the real work of art here is not a sculpture or a painting, but rather the architecture itself.

2004

Millau Viaduct

MILLAU, FRANCE

TEAMED WITH THE French engineers Sogelerg (Michel Virlogeux), EEG, and SERF, Norman Foster won a limited competition against French architects in 1996 to build a 1.55 mile (2.5 kilometer) viaduct on the A75 highway running between Clermont-Ferrand and Béziers, across the valley of the Tarn River. Long studied, this highway route was intended to alleviate excessive traffic in Millau during the holiday season. With columns varying in height from 246 to 804 feet (75 to 245 meters), the viaduct is a multispan cable-stayed design with sections each 1,148 feet (350 meters) in length. Opened in December 2004 after three years of construction, the viaduct cost approximately 400 million euros to build and created a certain controversy because it is the tallest bridge in the world, with one mast, the P2 pylon, reaching a height of 1,125 feet (343 meters). Local concern was raised that it threatened to dwarf the features of the countryside, and associations such as the World Wildlife Fund actively opposed the project. In fact, the controversy reached the highest levels of the French government. Valéry Giscard d'Estaing, the former president of France, went so far as to write to his successor Jacques Chirac, saying, "This project must elicit the most serious reservations, which is why I ask you to reexamine this question at your earliest convenience. . . . The project envisaged for Millau belongs to the family of cable-stayed bridges often built near the entries to ports or in the mouths of rivers. . . . In designing a bridge which spans a valley at such a great height, it is necessary to obtain a less opaque profile, which is less oppressive for the surrounding countryside." Giscard's intervention was not sufficient to reverse the decision that had been made to select Foster's scheme.

The completed structure boasts the highest road bridge deck in Europe, passing 886 feet (270 meters) above the Tarn River. Foster in this instance undertook a task that is often reserved for engineers. Such had also been the case in his earlier Torre de Collserola in Barcelona (1992), which measures 945 feet (288 meters) high. Foster is proud of the fact that a more conventional design for a tower of this height would have required a main support more than six times broader than the 14.8 foot (4.5 meter)

diameter hollow slip-formed reinforced concrete shaft, which reduces to just 11.8 inches (300 millimeters) to hold a radio mast. In the context of the Millau Viaduct, he says, "It is why some things which appear to be very simple, look better than others, whether it be aircraft, or bridges. You don't have to be an architect to have an eye, and I know lots of architects who don't have an eye. When you see a bridge that really sings, then you can be sure that that engineer had an eye. When you see one aircraft which is more remarkable than another, the same is true. They are all obeying the laws of nature. There are a whole series of visual options which permit one to achieve an optimal engineering solution, whether it is in designing a building, a bridge or an aircraft. You are making a choice. You are using an eye."

Wind tunnel testing did lead to slight modifications in the form of the bridge. But it cannot be denied that aside from all its technical superlatives, the bridge has an obvious elegance, hardly disturbing the natural setting that it crosses over and in a sense sublimating it, rendering it even more beautiful to those who drive across.

Millau Viaduct
Millau, France, 2004

The viaduct weighs approximately 290,000 tons and used roughly 127,000 cubic meters of concrete. High-grade steel was used to construct the bridge deck. Two thousand sections were constructed at the Alsace factory of the construction firm Eiffage and then placed in position using GPS technology.

2008

National Stadium

BEIJING, CHINA

THE ARCHITECTS Jacques Herzog and Pierre de Meuron were both born in Basel in 1950. They received degrees in architecture at the ETH Zurich in 1975, after studying with Aldo Rossi, and founded their firm Herzog & de Meuron Architecture Studio in Basel in 1978. They were chosen early in 1995 to turn the former Bankside Power Station, on the Thames opposite St. Paul's Cathedral, into Tate Modern, a museum for contemporary art that opened in May 2000. This commission immediately launched their international reputation, which has not faded since. With a site area of 50 acres (20 hectares) and a floor area of nearly 2.8 million square feet (258,000 square meters), the Main Stadium for the 2008 Olympic Games, not least because of its media exposure, is one of the most significant buildings of the early twenty-first century. The architects, who won a 2003 competition against twelve other submitting architects, collaborated with the Chinese artist Ai Weiwei on the project.

The client, the Beijing Public Works Authority, wanted a design that was not only new but "porous"—a "collective building and a public vessel." Nearly circular, the stadium sought to optimize viewing conditions for approximately 91,000 spectators handled during the Olympics. The removal of 11,000 temporary seats after the games gave the stadium a permanent capacity of 80,000 persons. As the architects described the structure: "The bowl superstructure consists of in-situ concrete. The primary structure of the roof is independent of the bowl structure and is conceived as a series of steel space frames wrapped around the bowl. The overall depth of the structure is 12 meters (39.37 feet). The spaces between the members are filled with ETFE foil." Careful attention was paid to airflows, the reuse of rain water, and cooling or heating via a system of pipes under the playing field. A retractable roof, part of the original

design, was removed from the brief after Chinese authorities reviewed the collapse of part of Terminal E at Charles de Gaulle Airport in Paris on May 23, 2004. This also reduced the overall cost of the facility.

Facade and structure are identical in this instance, in a form likened by the architects to a bird's nest of interwoven twigs. The structure was in fact nicknamed the Bird's Nest. As the architects write, "The spatial effect of the stadium is novel and radical and yet simple and of an almost archaic immediacy. Its appearance is pure structure." This stadium was the venue for the opening and closing ceremonies of the 2008 Olympic Games as well as for the subsequent Paralympic Games, and it was undoubtedly the most recognizable architectural "icon" related to that event. Although the stadium and the area around it were heralded as the most important public spaces in the Chinese capital at the time, in 2012, at the time of the London Olympic Games, the structure had no regular tenant, and the nearby Olympic Aquatics Center had been turned into a water park.

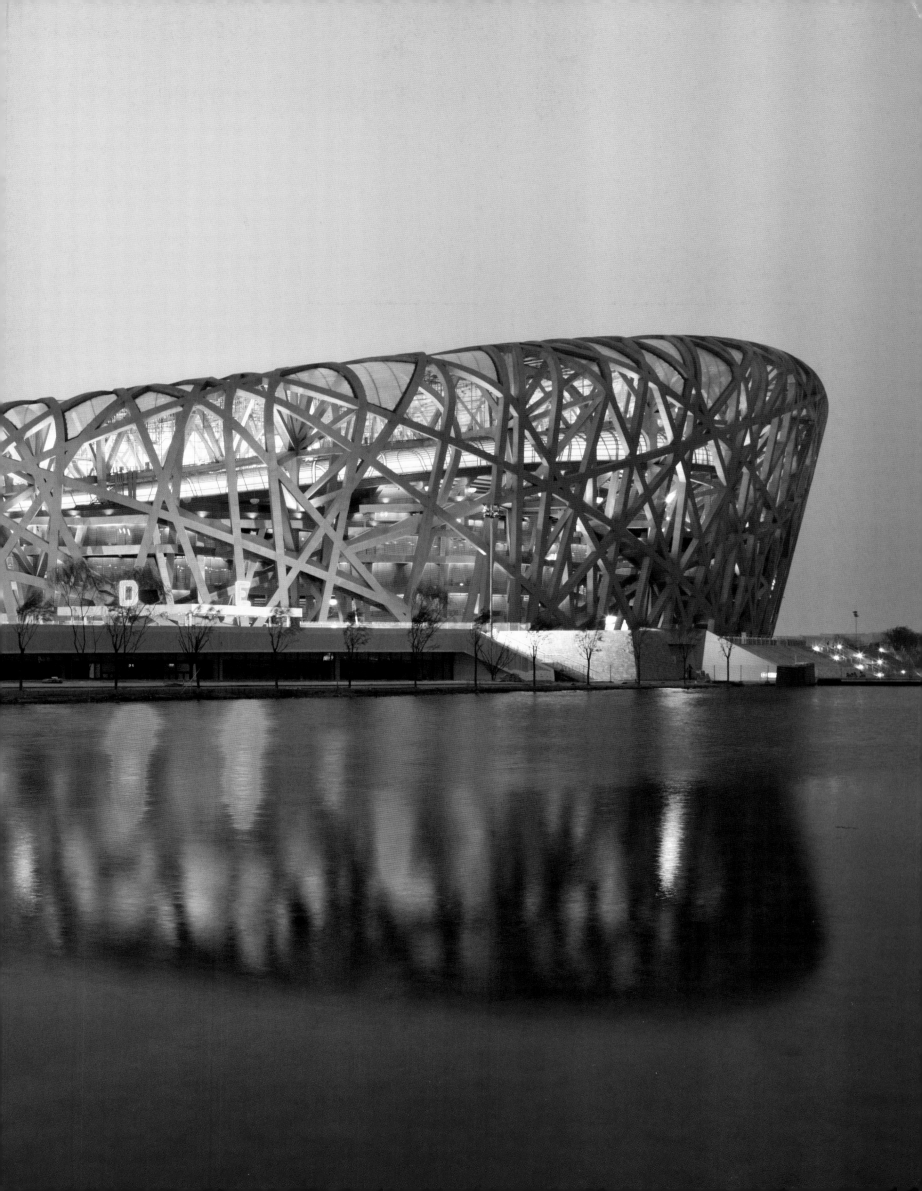

Index